WHAT WE REALLY VALUE

WHAT WE REALLY VALUE
Beyond Rubrics in Teaching and Assessing Writing

BOB BROAD

UTAH STATE UNIVERSITY PRESS
Logan, Utah

Utah State University Press
Logan, Utah 84322-7800

Manufactured in the United States of America
Cover design by Barbara Yale-Read
Cover illustration "World Map" by Pietro Vesconte (c. 1321), courtesy of
the British Library Board, London.
"Vinland Map" (c. 1440) in Prologue, courtesy of Yale University Library, New Haven.

Library of Congress Cataloging-in-Publication Data
Broad, Bob, 1960-
  What we really value : beyond rubrics in teaching and assessing
writing / Bob Broad.
      p. cm.
Includes bibliographical references (p.) and index.
  ISBN 0-87421-553-6 (pbk. : alk. paper)
  1. English language—Rhetoric—Study and teaching. 2. Report
writing—Study and teaching (Higher) 3. English language—Ability
testing. 4. Grading and marking (Students) 5. Report
writing—Evaluation. I. Title.
  PE1404 .B738 2003
  808'.042'0711—dc21
                    2002153374

for
JULIE SUZANNE HILE
my finest friend, partner, and teacher

and for
DYLAN AND RACHEL
who make everything so much more worthwhile

in memory of
MAURICE SCHARTON
teacher, colleague, writing assessment dude

CONTENTS

LIST OF FIGURES

LIST OF TABLES

PROLOGUE

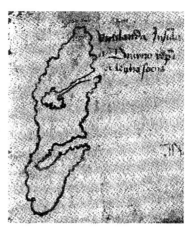

In chapter 3 of *Drawing the Line: Tales of Maps and Cartocontroversy* (1995), Mark Monmonier tells the story of the Vinland Map. Released to the public for the first time in 1965, this map appears to demonstrate that Vikings not only visited what we now call North America centuries before Columbus but also *mapped* that continent, which would make them—as far as we know—the first in history to have done so. What interests map specialists most about the Vinland Map is whether it is a genuine fifteenth-century document or a flamboyant twentieth-century forgery. And after thirty years of debunkings and rebunkings, cartographers still don't agree on this point.[i]

Luckily, I am not a cartographer, but a teacher and scholar of rhetoric with a special interest in writing assessment. I am therefore free to take a different sort of interest in the Vinland Map. It fascinates me as a dramatic example of representation based on what we would now consider woefully inadequate inquiry and information. Yet the cartography of the Vinland Map was quite sufficient to the time and purpose for which it was produced.[ii]

As early as 985 CE, Vikings explored the western reaches of the North Atlantic Ocean, including parts of North America. In the early fifteenth century, the Roman Catholic Church wanted to establish the scope of "Christendom," its spiritual and material empire. On the basis of the Vikings' explorations, the holy mapmakers were able to offer the following information about the Church's western frontier in the form of the Vinland Map:

1. There's land over there.
2. It's a very big piece of land, even bigger than Greenland.

    3.   It has a couple of big bays on its east coast.

    4.   It's ours to claim.

I want to emphasize two aspects of this information. First, all these claims but the last was true, though the vast data they omit makes them seem ludicrous. Second, for the time in which it was composed and the purposes to which it was put, the Vinland Map served perfectly well. Only from our twenty-first-century point of view as inhabitants or neighbors of North America does the Vinland Map appear bizarrely inaccurate and useless. For people who need to live, work, or travel in North America, the Vinland Map does not suffice.

Now consider the familiar five- or six-point list found on most "rubrics" or "scoring guides" for writing assessment. These documents claim to represent a teacher's or writing program's rhetorical values, the qualities and characteristics for which readers reward or penalize authors. A currently popular example of a traditional rubric is Northwest Regional Educational Laboratory's "6+1 Trait Writing" framework.

    1.   Ideas

    2.   Organization

    3.   Voice

    4.   Word Choice

    5.   Sentence Fluency

    6.   Conventions

    7.   Presentation

        (2001)

Such concise lists of criteria may have adequately served the needs of writing assessment for forty years by making judgments simple, quick, and agreeable. As a guide to how texts are actually composed, read, interpreted, and valued, however, I propose that traditional rubrics are as dangerously unsatisfactory for purposes of contemporary rhetoric and composition as the Vinland Map would have been to Lewis and Clark or to someone wishing to travel Route 66 from Chicago to Los Angeles. My book proposes a method of inquiry into and negotiation of rhetorical values in classrooms and writing programs that should liberate composition from reliance on such Vinland Maps. After all, we live here.

NOTES

i. Type "Vinland Map" into your web search engine to find illustrations and discussions of the map.

ii. This Prologue discusses the Vinland Map, which is quite different from the map adorning the cover of this book. On the cover is pictured Pietro Vesconte's beautiful World Map, composed circa 1321. The key similarity between these two earliest world maps is their incompleteness and inaccuracy by contemporary standards. The key difference is that the Vinland Map pictures what we now call North America, though in an unrecognizable form. North and South America are entirely missing from Vesconte's map of the world, for he lacked the knowledge required to chart them.

ACKNOWLEDGMENTS

This book grows out of work done by dozens of people, some of whom I must thank by name here. My apologies in advance to any comrades I may have inadvertently omitted from this list.

Tom Gerschick was my steadfast, weekly writing-mate for the seven years leading up to this book's completion. He and Georgeanne Rundblad devoted years to nurturing my spirits and scholarship in our writing group, "Left to Write." As my life-partner, Julie Hile could not escape "invitations" to read draft upon draft of whatever I might be writing; nevertheless she did so with a generous spirit and radiant intelligence. The following people not only read the prospectus of, or chapters from, this book and offered helpful suggestions for improvement, they also produced scholarship and set professional examples that helped make my entire project possible: Richard Haswell, Brian Huot, Michael Neal, Lee Nickoson-Massey, Peggy O'Neill, Ellen Schendel, and Mike Williamson. Slightly removed but equally important role models, mentors, and supporters include: Paul Anderson, Marcia Baxter-Magolda, Don Daiker, Jennie Dautermann, Peter Elbow, Ron Fortune, Maggy Lindgren, Pam Moss, Kathleen Yancey, and Ed White. Special thanks go to Susanmarie Harrington and Ellen Schendel for writing reviews that significantly improved the text.

Yvonna S. Lincoln, whom I've never met, once said at a conference that "We [qualitative researchers] need to collect fewer data and do more with the data we collect"; thus she gave me confidence to mine the City University data for years. Illinois State University's Department of English and College of Arts and Sciences provided invaluable *time* for research and writing in the form of moderate teaching load and a sabbatical. With his grace, wit, efficiency, intelligence, and humor, Michael Spooner spoils authors who publish with Utah State University Press. Finally I want to acknowledge the students, faculty, and administrators at City University: after a decade or so of pseudonymizing you and analyzing (every which way) your groundbreaking work in teaching and assessing writing, I am pleased to announce that I am (I believe) now finished with you so we can all move on with our lives.

In writing this book, I have been gifted with the support and encouragement of many friends and colleagues. Perhaps the single most heartening thing I heard was that readers believed my book could make a difference, that it would prove useful in the hands of students, teachers, administrators, and scholars of writing. To emphasize this point, one reviewer concluded her written discussion of my book with a transcription of Marge Piercy's poem "To Be of Use" (1982).

If these predictions prove true and my book turns out to be useful, then I will feel rewarded beyond measure. For now, I wish to re-direct that reviewer's poetic tribute into a blessing on my readers and the good they will do with the book. May *What We Really Value* help you make the work you do—learning, teaching, and assessing composition—more satisfying and more real.

> . . . the thing worth doing well done
> has a shape that satisfies, clean and evident.
> ***
> The pitcher cries for water to carry
> and a person for work that is real.

1

TO TELL THE TRUTH
Beyond Rubrics

College writing research in the disciplinary period which began, roughly, in the mid-1960s has not told us much about exactly what it is that teachers value in student writing. Researchers who have used statistical methodologies to address this question have thrown little light on the issue. . . . And guidelines published by English departments—at least at places where I've taught—are even less specific. An "A" paper is one that "displays unusual competence"; hence, an "A" paper is an "A" paper.
FAIGLEY, *Fragments of Rationality*

Consider your favorite college or university writing program. Instructors in the program may include tenure-line faculty, adjunct faculty, graduate teaching assistants, and an administrator or two. Some are new to the program; some have been there thirty years. Several of them are trained in the field of composition and teach it by choice; others teach writing only when they can't teach literature; a few are on the writing staff mainly because it's a paying job. This diverse troupe probably delivers one or two required introductory composition courses to nearly every student who appears at your institution's door. Though they diverge considerably in their backgrounds, emphases, interests, and areas of expertise in teaching rhetoric, your program's instructors almost certainly teach a clearly established curriculum, including common readings, writing assignments, writing processes, and educational goals.

Now ask yourself about these teachers of college composition the question Lester Faigley implies in the epigraph above: What exactly do they value in their students' writing? More likely than not, your writing program's best answer will be found in a rubric or scoring guide, the "guidelines published by English departments" Faigley mentions. Hundreds of such guides for writing assessment are available in books and on the worldwide web, and many writing programs have their own. A prominent example can be found in the back of Edward M. White's *Teaching and Assessing Writing* (298). White's "Sample Holistic Scoring Guide" ("prepared by committees in the California State University

English departments, 1988") identifies six levels of rhetorical achievement. At CSU, a student's text qualifies for the highest rating ("superior") if it meets the following five criteria:

> Addresses the question fully and explores the issues thoughtfully
> Shows substantial depth, fullness, and complexity of thought
> Demonstrates clear, focused, unified, and coherent organization
> Is fully developed and detailed
> Evidences superior control of diction, syntactic variety, and transition; may have a few minor flaws

As a statement of the key rhetorical values of CSU English departments, I find this guide admirable in its clarity, simplicity, and emphasis on intellectual and rhetorical substance over surface mechanics or format concerns. Furthermore, by presenting not only levels of achievement ("incompetent" to "superior") but also the five specific evaluative criteria quoted above, it goes far beyond the tautological "A = A" formulation that Faigley protests.

But does it go far enough? The strength of the hundreds of rubrics like White's lies in what they include; their great weakness is what they leave out. They present to the world several inarguably important criteria endorsed by the local writing program administrator as the criteria by which writing should be evaluated in the relevant program. They omit any mention of the dozens of other criteria (such as "interest," "tone," or "legibility") by which any rhetorical performance is also likely to be judged. In pursuit of their *normative* and *formative* purposes, traditional rubrics achieve evaluative brevity and clarity. In so doing, they surrender their *descriptive* and *informative* potential: responsiveness, detail, and complexity in accounting for how writing is actually evaluated.

We need to critically examine such representations of our rhetorical values on the basis of what they teach—and fail to teach—students, faculty, and the public about the field of writing instruction. Theories of learning, composition, and writing assessment have evolved to the point at which the method and technology of the rubric now appear dramatically at odds with our ethical, pedagogical, and political commitments. In short, traditional rubrics and scoring guides prevent us from telling the truth about what we believe, what we teach, and what we value in composition courses and programs.

Theorists of knowledge from Nietzsche to Foucault and beyond have taught us that calls for "truth" cannot go unexplained. So I propose this working definition of *truth* as I use it in this book: truth means *doing our epistemological best.* Before we make a knowledge claim (for example, Here is how writing is valued in our writing program) that carries with it serious consequences for students, faculty, and society, we need to conduct the best inquiry we can. In their rush toward clarity, simplicity, brevity, and authority, traditional scoring guides make substantial knowledge claims based on inadequate research.

A prime assumption of my work is that a teacher of writing cannot provide an adequate account of his rhetorical values just by sitting down and reflecting on them; neither can a WPA provide an adequate account of the values of her writing program by thinking about them or even by talking about them in general terms with her writing instructors. In this book I offer what I believe is a method of evaluative inquiry better grounded both theoretically and empirically, a method that yields a more satisfactory process of exploration and a more useful representation of the values by which we teach and assess writing.

WHAT WE REALLY TEACH

As a subfield of English studies, rhetoric and composition teaches and researches what educators generally accept as the preeminent intellectual skills of the university: critical and creative thinking, as well as interpretation, revision, and negotiation of texts and of the knowledge those texts are used to create (Berlin). Done well, this work prepares our students for success in personal relationships, careers, and democratic citizenship.

Most of us in the field would therefore likely embrace as part of our mission Marcia Baxter Magolda's call to help students move toward "self-authorship," defined as "the ability to collect, interpret, and analyze information and reflect on one's own beliefs in order to form judgments" (14). Unfortunately, the undergraduate experiences of participants in Baxter Magolda's study mainly lacked conditions that would have helped them develop in such sophisticated ways. As a result, during their early postcollege careers, they often struggled and stumbled in their efforts to "become the authors of their own lives." Reflecting on what higher education did and did not offer her study's participants, Baxter Magolda explains:

> They would have been better prepared for these [early interpersonal, career, and citizenship] roles, and have struggled less, had the conditions for self-authorship been created during their college experience. (xxii)

The key academic principle that helps students move toward self-authorship is, according to Baxter Magolda, *"that knowledge is complex, ambiguous, and socially constructed in a context"* (195, Baxter Magolda's emphasis). Theory, research, and teaching in rhetoric and composition strongly support such views of knowledge, including its social and context-specific character. However, rubrics, the most visible and ubiquitous tool of *writing assessment*—arguably the aspect of rhetoric/composition that impinges most powerfully and memorably on our students' lives—teach our students an exactly opposite view of knowledge, judgment, and value. At the heart of our educational and rhetorical project, rubrics are working against us.

For all its achievements and successes over the past half century (see Yancey), the field of writing assessment has no adequate method for answering one of its most urgent and important questions: What do we value in our students' writing? What we have instead are rubrics and scoring guides that "over-emphasize formal, format, or superficial-trait characteristics" of composition (Wiggins 132) and that present "generalized, synthetic representations of [rhetorical] performances . . . too generic for describing, analyzing, and explaining individual performances" (Delandshere and Petrosky 21). Instead of a process of inquiry and a document that would highlight for our students the complexity, ambiguity, and context-sensitivity of rhetorical evaluation, we have presented our students with a process and document born long ago of a very different need: to make assessment quick, simple, and agreeable. In the field of writing assessment, increasing demands for truthfulness, usefulness, and meaningfulness are now at odds with the requirements of efficiency and standardization. The age of the rubric has passed.

Regarding rubrics and scoring guides everywhere, I raise questions not only about their content but also about their origins and uses. To determine what we really value in a particular writing program, we must therefore pursue several related questions:

> How do we discover what we really value?
> How do we negotiate differences and shifts in what we value?
> How do we represent what we have agreed to value? and
> What difference do our answers to these questions make?

Compositionists willing to address these questions of inquiry, negotiation, representation, and consequences, will, I believe, find traditional rubrics and scoring guides lacking crucial ethical, pedagogical, and political qualities. This book points the way toward a new method for discovering, negotiating, and publicizing *what we really value* in students' writing. We can reclaim what rhetoric and composition lost half a century ago when it adopted rubrics and scoring guides as its preeminent method of representing a writing program's rhetorical values.

THE BIRTH OF RUBRICS

Modern writing assessment was born in 1961 in Princeton, New Jersey. That year, Diederich, French, and Carlton of the Educational Testing Service (ETS) published *Factors in Judgments of Writing Ability* (ETS Research Bulletin 61-15). Basing their work on nearly a decade of research already done (at ETS and elsewhere) on writing assessment generally and especially on inter-rater agreement, Diederich, French, and Carlton declared that

> The purpose of this study was to serve as a stepping stone toward closer agreement among judges of student writing . . . by revealing common causes of disagreement [among those judges]. ("Abstract")

Though the coauthors of the study emphasized that "It was not the purpose of this study to achieve a high degree of unanimity among the readers but [rather] to reveal the differences of opinion that prevail in uncontrolled grading—both in the academic community and in the educated public," still they found themselves "disturbed" by the wide variability in scoring among their fifty-three "distinguished readers": "[I]t was disturbing to find that 94% of the [300] papers received either seven, eight, or nine of the nine possible grades; that no paper received less than five different grades; and that the median correlation between readers was .31" (Abstract). The next half-century of research and practice in writing assessment was definitively charted in the single word "disturbing." Diederich, French, and Carlton had purposefully set out to investigate the geography, if you will, of rhetorical values among fifty-three "educated and intelligent" readers in six fields. Yet the truth they revealed "disturbed" them. Why? Because within the world of positivist psychometrics, the world in which ETS and other commercial testing corporations still operate, precise agreement among judges is taken as the preeminent measure of the validity of an assessment. Therefore, rather than seek to understand and carefully map out the swampy, rocky, densely forested terrain of writing assessment that they found lying before them, they quickly moved to simplify and standardize it thus:

A classification of comments was developed by taking readers at random and writing captions under which their comments could be classified until no further types of comments could be found. After many changes, 55 categories of comments were adopted and arranged under seven main headings:

1. Ideas
2. Style
3. Organization
4. Paragraphing
5. Sentence structure
6. Mechanics
7. Verbal facility

(Diederich, French, and Carlton 21)

Using factor analysis—one of the "statistical methodologies" Faigley views with skepticism—the ETS researchers eventually derived from those seven main headings a list of five "factors" that seemed to capture the values of their readers:

Ideas: relevance, clarity, quantity, development, persuasiveness
Form: organization and analysis
Flavor: style, interest, sincerity
Mechanics: specific errors in punctuation, grammar, etc.
Wording: choice and arrangement of words

And thus was born what became the standard, traditional, five-point rubric, by some version of which nearly every large-scale assessment of writing since 1961 has been strictly guided.

Two things leap off every page of *Factors in Judgments of Writing Ability:* the analytical and imaginative genius of the researchers and their sure command of methods of statistical analysis, most especially factor analysis. What is less obvious is that, because they were firmly committed to the positivist, experimentalist paradigm that ruled their day, they let a historic opportunity slip away. Confronted with an apparent wilderness of rhetorical values, they retreated to a simplified, ordered, well-controlled representation that would keep future writing assessment efforts clean of such disturbing features as dissent, diversity, context-sensitivity, and ambiguity. Three centuries earlier, officials of the Catholic Church turned away from Galileo's telescope, so "disturbed" by what it showed them that they refused to look into it again. After showing the astronomer the Church's instruments of torture to inspire his recantation and subsequent silence, they returned eagerly to Ptolemy's comfortingly familiar millennium-old map of the heavens showing earth as the motionless center of the universe.

Within the paradigms of positivist psychometrics (Moss 1994) and experimentalist methods (North), dramatic evaluative disagreements like the ones Diederich, French, and Carlton carefully documented must necessarily register as failures. Disagreement is failure because positivism presumes a stable and independent reality (in this case "writing ability" or "writing quality") that humans try more or less successfully to "measure." The fact that "94% of the papers [in their study] received either seven, eight, or nine of the nine possible grades," was "disturbing" because if evaluators had been free of "error" and "idiosyncrasy" (Diederich's terms), they would have agreed in their judgments. The obvious psychometric solution to the problem of disagreement is to rebuild readers' evaluative frameworks so they can agree more consistently and more quickly. From the beginning this has been the precise purpose of the scoring guide and rubric, and these tools have served us well: when we use them, we can reach impressively high correlations among scorers, and we can judge students' writing with remarkable speed and relative ease.

From the standpoint of a constructivist or rhetorical paradigm, however, Diederich, French, and Carlton's achievement seems more *scientistic* than scientific. That is, it seems to provide an abstracted, idealized representation and to take on the appearance of objective truth by turning away from the messy facts at hand. Their epistemological frame and their statistical methods prevented them from delving into the powerful knowledge they revealed and clearly stated in their report: the "empirical fact" that

> If [readers'] grades do not agree, it is not for lack of interest, knowledge, or sensitivity, but because competent readers with their diversity of background will genuinely differ in tastes and standards. (10)

The 1961 study by Diederich, French, and Carlton created an opportunity to chart in detail the axiological terrain of writing assessment among this group of "distinguished readers." The ETS team of researchers achieved the chance to show the world what real experts working in real professions in the real world valued in real college students' writing. This is the truth and the reality they discovered, and it could have provided them and us with a powerful authority and reference point for understanding writing assessment. Their positivist presuppositions and methods, however, compelled them in a different direction. Decrying their findings as "disturbing" and full of evaluators' "error," Diederich, French, and Carlton traded in the rhetorical truth confronting them (that readers value texts differently) in exchange for the grail of high inter-rater agreement. It is now time to trade back the grail and reclaim the truth.

First, however, we should acknowledge the benefits rubrics brought us during their fifty-year ascendancy. In the historical context of U.S. culture in 1961 and the following decades, rubrics may have done more good for writing assessment and the teaching of writing than any other concept or technology. During a time when educators were under constant pressure to judge "writing" ability using multiple-choice tests of grammar knowledge, the work of Diederich, French, and Carlton (and other researchers at ETS and elsewhere) legitimized direct assessment of writing (assessment that took actual *writing* as the object of judgment). In the 1960s, to become acceptable and legitimate, writing assessment first had to prove itself "scientific." And scientificness, in the context of positivist psychometrics, required a level of standardization and agreement that would provide the impression that the thing being judged—in this case *writing ability*—was indeed an objective "thing." If readers disagreed significantly—as Diederich's study resoundingly proved they did—then the procedure was by definition "unscientific." This is why Diederich, French, and Carlton treated their "empirical facts" showing the fabulous richness and complexity of rhetorical values merely as a "stepping stone" toward a cleaner, clearer, more agreeable representation of the judgment of writing. First and foremost, then, rubrics bought writing assessment legitimacy.

But that's not all. Streamlining and reducing the possibilities for rhetorical judgment also speeded up what every writing teacher knows to be a mind-numbing and time-devouring task. So just as the agreeability rubrics promoted brought us legitimacy, the increased speed they provided brought us affordability. When time and money are short—as they always are in education—rubrics provide badly needed relief and enable faculty to assign and judge actual writing from large numbers of students with relative speed and ease.

Scoring guides yielded yet another set of advantages: documentation of the process of evaluating writing. Notoriously obscure in nature, the judgment of writing quality was at last explained in clear, simple, and public terms, so judgments could be held accountable to the values specified in the rubric. Students, instructors, and the general public could hold in their hands a clear framework for discussing, teaching, and assessing writing. As public records of rhetorical values, rubrics made writing assessment less capricious.

Legitimacy, affordability, and accountability— these are the gifts brought to our field in 1961 by Diederich, French, and Carlton and by the rubrics they helped establish as a permanent fixture in large-scale writing assessment.

BEYOND RUBRICS

The 1990s brought dramatic changes to the fields of psychometrics and writing assessment. In this new theoretical context, we can look at rubrics with fresh eyes and raise critical questions about them that should open up new possibilities for writing assessment.

The key developments are in the area of validity theory. Because other scholars of assessment (Huot 1996; Moss 1992; Williamson; Yancey) have already addressed these changes in detail, I will touch on them only briefly before focusing on their implications for rubrics and for the practice of writing assessment beyond rubrics.

Assessment has become a public and educational issue, not solely a technical one. We no longer seem to be content to be told that assessments meet certain psychometric and statistical requirements. We want to know whether they help or hurt learning and teaching. Delandshere and Petrosky provide an apt synopsis of this shift in assessment theory:

> In the last few years, there has been a shift in the rhetoric (if not yet the practice) of assessment (e.g., Gipps, 1994; Resnick & Resnick, 1992; Shepard, 1989; Wiggins, 1993; Wolf, Bixby, Glenn, & Gardner, 1991). Much more emphasis has been placed on the support of learning and teaching than on the sorting and ranking of individuals. (15)

To put it another way, researchers, theorists, and practitioners have joined together in their refusal to ignore the educational impact of assessments. As Wiggins states,

> In performance tests of writing we are too often sacrificing validity for reliability; we sacrifice insight for efficiency; we sacrifice authenticity for ease of scoring. Assessments should improve performance (and insight into authentic performance), not just audit it. (129)

These researchers have thrown off positivist-psychometric prohibitions against considering contextual factors and thus have been willing to challenge assessment practices that appear to undermine or corrupt best educational practices.

The key flashpoint in this controversy has been the issue of inter-rater agreement (a key aspect of "reliability") and its relationship to validity. Moss addressed the question bluntly in the title of her essay "Can There Be Validity Without Reliability?" (Moss 1994). Her answer to that question is a qualified "yes." Moss and others rely in turn for much of their argument on the work of psychometricians Lee J. Cronbach and Samuel Messick. On key validity issues, these theorists of evaluation have argued, for example, that "validity" is not a quality of an assessment instrument (a test or a portfolio assessment, for example), but rather a quality of the *decisions* people make on the basis of such instruments. This claim takes validity out of the technical realm to which psychometrics had relegated (and thus controlled) it for decades and puts it back into the realm of public discourse, in which anyone could speak to the educational effects and conceptual integrity of an assessment and thus to its validity.

Arguing for a "unified theory of validity," Michael Neal (building on the work of Huot, Williamson, and others) presents five different issues that must be considered in assessing validity:

1. criterion-related validity
2. reliability [especially inter-rater agreement]
3. traditional construct validity
4. content validity
5. social consequences

(Neal 2002)

The key point here for my study is that validity has become more broadly and more multiply defined, and this has opened up new avenues of discussion, debate, and inquiry.

Grant Wiggins raises a particularly strong voice in the struggle to broaden and humanize assessment issues and, especially, validity, in his article "The Constant Danger of Sacrificing Validity to Reliability: Making Writing Assessment Serve Writers." As the title makes clear, Wiggins takes part in a shift in validity theory away from nearly exclusive attention to inter-rater agreement (the chief consideration to which Diederich and his colleagues were devoted) and toward concerns driven by his core argument, that "Tests themselves teach." The crucial question then becomes "What do our assessments teach?"

The fact is that almost all writing assessments I have seen use rubrics that stress compliance with rules about writing as opposed to the real purpose of writing, namely, the power and insight of the words. Writing rubrics in every district and state over-emphasize formal, format, or superficial-trait characteristics. (132)

The net effect of this validity revolution is to shift attention to the broad impact of assessments on teaching and learning and to judge the appropriateness of assessments based on the outcomes of high-stakes decisions affecting students' lives.

These recent shifts in validity theory cast writing assessment—especially rubrics and scoring guides—in a different light from that in which Diederich and his followers saw them. In 1961, agreement was the only discernible path to proving the legitimacy of direct writing assessment. Half a century later, in great part thanks to the work of Diederich, French, and Carlton and their followers, most assessment specialists (even those who work for testing corporations) support direct writing assessment. With a growing focus on the importance of connecting assessment to teaching and tapping into the pedagogical and epistemological value of differences among readers, Diederich's turn away from the disturbing complexity of real readers toward the standardized and simplified portrait presented by the rubric takes on new meanings.

Consider the validity double bind in which scoring guides necessarily find themselves. Remember that the function of the guide is to focus and narrow the factors or criteria by which readers judge in order to boost efficiency and agreeability. Whether the guide succeeds or fails in this task, it precipitates a crisis of validity in the assessment.

If, as often appears to be the case (Charney; Delandshere and Petrosky), the guide is "successful" in streamlining the messy mix of rhetorical values instructors bring to communal writing assessment, then that evaluation judges students according to values different from those by which instructors have taught and assessed writing in their classrooms. Therefore, the shared evaluation diverges from the "real" values of the writing program as enacted by the program's instructors in the program's classrooms. For the assessment to be relevant, valid, and fair, however, it must judge students according to the same skills and values by which they have been taught.

If, on the other hand, as other researchers have shown (Barritt, Stock, and Clark; Huot 1993), scoring guides often fail to narrow and standardize the values by which teachers judge students' writing, then they significantly misrepresent the values at work in the writing program (both in classrooms and in the shared assessment process). In this case the scoring guide represents not what instructors value in students' writing, but rather what someone believes the program's rhetorical values to be, or what someone wants them to be, or what someone wants people to believe them to be. The rubric claims to represent the evaluative terrain of the program, but at the very best it documents only a small fraction of the rhetorical values at work there.

So rubrics may or may not succeed in narrowing the range of criteria by which we judge student's writing. The problem is that *either way,* they fail important tests of validity and ethics. Still we lack a rigorous, detailed, and accurate account of what instructors in the program value in teaching and assessing writing.

Not only as a document does the rubric or scoring guide fall short. It also fails us as a process of inquiry. Very rarely do rubrics emerge from an open and systematic inquiry into a writing program's values. Instead, they are most often drafted by an individual (usually the writing program administrator) and approved by a committee before being delivered into the hands of evaluators as the official and authoritative guide to judging students' writing. By predetermining criteria for evaluation, such a process shuts down the open discussion and debate among professional teachers of writing that communal writing assessment should provide. Delandshere and Petrosky describe the problem this way:

> Ratings "force fit" performances into general categories; they mold them into abstractions that are defined solely to create scores and score variance, but they do not seem very helpful in describing or explaining the particulars of any one performance. As such, ratings are poor representations of complex events and, given the generic nature of the scoring rubrics, the danger exists that the assessors will attend to the most visible or superficial characteristics of the performance while neglecting the specific patterns and connections that give it meaning and integrity. (21)

More open and meaningful discussion and debate would not only improve the quality and legitimacy of the resulting document, but would also provide participants with one of the most powerful opportunities for professional development available to teachers of writing.

Instructors, administrators, and researchers of writing, as well as our students, our colleagues elsewhere in the academy, and the general public, all deserve both a rigorous inquiry into what we really value and a detailed document recording the results of that inquiry. This book advocates a new method of evaluative exploration, demonstrates that method in the context of one university's writing program, highlights the method's usefulness to other writing programs, and suggests specific actions for instructors and administrators of composition who wish to move beyond rubrics to more robust truths about teaching and assessing writing.

DYNAMIC CRITERIA MAPPING

Having argued that positivist psychometrics and its scoring guides have cost writing instruction a great deal, I now propose an alternative method for inquiring into and documenting how we really evaluate our students' texts. The method I recommend and demonstrate in this book I have named "Dynamic Criteria Mapping." Dynamic Criteria Mapping (DCM) is a streamlined form of qualitative inquiry that yields a detailed, complex, and useful portrait of any writing program's evaluative dynamics. Later chapters provide a detailed example of the results of this form of inquiry, as well as recommendations for specific DCM strategies. Here I will explain the theoretical background for the method.

The interplay between two forms of educational inquiry, writing assessment and qualitative research, has gained increasing attention lately in books and journals devoted to improving postsecondary teaching and learning. Scholars in a variety of fields—composition and rhetoric (Huot 1996), evaluation theory (Moss 1996), and qualitative research (Guba and Lincoln)—have directed researchers' attention to the benefits of integrating qualitative methods into educational evaluation.

In *(Re)Articulating Writing Assessment for Teaching and Learning,* Huot outlines six principles that inform what he sees as the coming wave of writing assessment practices. Huot foresees that the new generation of assessment programs will be

1. Site-based
2. Locally controlled
3. Context-sensitive
4. Rhetorically based
5. Accessible

(178)

These five principles clash dramatically with those of positivist psychometrics, which privileges instead generalizability, context-independence, statistical analysis, secrecy, and control (see "Beyond Rubrics" section above). Huot's five principles also correspond closely to the features that set qualitative research off from the dominant, experimentalist paradigm. Especially in his call for a grounding in rhetoric and a sensitivity to context, Huot touches on the key distinguishing features of interpretive research. In other words, when Huot predicted an impending (now ongoing) historical shift away from positivist psychometrics in evaluation, he simultaneously predicted the ascendance of qualitative methodology in writing assessment.

Pamela A. Moss, a prominent theorist of educational evaluation, calls for a shift in methods quite similar to Huot's. Distinguishing between a "naturalistic conception of social science" and an "interpretive conception," Moss advocates for including interpretive research methods in educational assessment.

> A second way in which interpretive research traditions might inform assessment theory and practice is by providing theory, illustrations, and methodologies that illuminate a complex social reality, thus enabling us to better understand the ways that assessments work within the local context. (1996, 27)

And Guba and Lincoln, in their landmark *Fourth Generation Evaluation*, make a similar argument. Here they explain why they term their approach to evaluation a "constructivist" one.

> The term *constructivist* is used to designate the methodology actually employed in doing an evaluation. It has its roots in an inquiry paradigm that is an alternative to the scientific paradigm, and we choose to call it the *constructivist* but it has many other names including *interpretive* and *hermeneutic*. (39 Guba and Lincoln's emphases)

These authors have pointed to a shift in assessment theory and practice toward an interpretive or qualitative paradigm. To date, however, the effort has remained mainly theoretical, and the limited application of such methods to writing assessment has been conducted by researchers, not practitioners.

The field of composition needs a workable method (supported by a well-developed theory) by which instructors and administrators in writing programs can discover, negotiate, and publicize the rhetorical values they employ when judging students' writing. Huot, Moss, and Guba and Lincoln have clearly called for this need to be satisfied by combining assessment theory and practice with qualitative research. Grounding these scholars' proposed integrative project in my study of a specific university's first-year writing program, I demonstrate and propose such a method: Dynamic Criteria Mapping.

The following chapter, "Studying Rubric-Free Assessment at City University: Research Context and Methods," introduces a distinctive first-year writing program featuring a portfolio assessment system that was, at the time of my field research, metamorphosing from the psychometric paradigm to a hermeneutic one (see Broad 2000). Several progressive elements in this program—including the absence of a scoring guide or rubric—made possible my inquiry into rhetorical values and the construction of the DCM model. Chapter 2 also describes my research methods, which extend from Glaser and Strauss's grounded theory approach Chapters 3 and 4 ("Textual Criteria" and "Contextual Criteria") present the findings that emerged from my study of what they really valued at City University. Chapter 5, "A Model for Dynamic Criteria Mapping of Communal Writing Assessment," highlights the benefits of DCM and offers specific suggestions for writing programs that wish to take up the sort of inquiry advocated here.

I aim to engage readers in questions of truth and method in program-wide writing assessment, persuade them of the need for change, and demonstrate specific techniques that will solve urgent problems we currently face. The immediate outcome should be a more productive process of evaluative inquiry and negotiation as well as a more detailed, accurate, and useful document to result from that inquiry. The long-term outcome should be better learning for students of composition, enhanced professional development for writing instructors, and increased leverage with the public for writing programs that can publicize a complex and compelling portrait of what they teach and value in students' writing.

2
STUDYING RUBRIC-FREE
ASSESSMENT AT CITY UNIVERSITY
Research Context and Methods

For two reasons, readers need to know about the portfolio program at City University and how I studied it. First, the numerous references to sample texts, specific events, and individuals at City University that run through my findings (presented in Chapters 3 and 4) would be difficult to understand and evaluate without a clear picture of both the portfolio program's elements and my grounded theory research methodology. Second, the streamlined version of Dynamic Criteria Mapping I recommend in Chapter 5 for all college and university writing programs is based directly on the full-fledged qualitative inquiry described here. The current chapter therefore describes in some detail both context and methods for my research.

This investigation draws on data I collected in the early 1990s. Those same data have formed the basis for several other studies (Broad 1997, 2000, and 1994b). Though the research questions and the analysis of data in this book differ significantly from those of the earlier studies, the data gathering and most of the theoretical background for my method overlap the earlier work. I have therefore adapted portions of previous discussions of context and methods for use in the current explanation. I encourage readers who seek greater methodological detail to see the earlier studies. [1]

RESEARCH CONTEXT: CITY UNIVERSITY'S WRITING PORTFOLIO PROGRAM

With the exception of my own name, all names of participants and institutions in this study are fictitious, including the name "City University." To protect participants' anonymity, I have also altered a small number of other nonessential facts about the program I studied. The widespread quoting of words and phrases in this book results from my effort to develop the analysis emically, that is, by drawing it out of the words and concepts of my research participants. Readers should therefore understand any quoted words not attributed to a specific source (in chapter headings, for example) to be quotations from observations, interviews, or documents at City University.

City University was a large, urban-Midwestern, publicly funded, research university. The College of Arts and Sciences housed the Department of English, which in turn housed the First-Year English (FYE) Program. Nearly all of the roughly four thousand students enrolled each year in the FYE course sequence—English 1, 2, and 3—were in their first year of study at City University. During the fall quarter in which I conducted my study, only three out of fifty English 1 instructors (6 percent) were full-time tenured or tenure-line faculty members; the remaining instructors (94 percent) were adjuncts and teaching assistants (TAs).

The portfolio assessment program I studied was an integral part of the first course in the FYE sequence, English 1. Described in program documents as a course in "writing about personal experience" and in "public discourse," English 1 lasted ten weeks and required students to compose essays on five topics or genres:

A significant event

A portrait (often referred to by instructors as the "significant person" assignment)

Problem/solution essay

Evaluation (written in a single class period, often taking the form of a review of a cultural event) and

Profile ("a description of a specific person, place, or activity")

(For details on these assignments, see appendix A, "Assignments for English 1 Essays.") Out of these five compositions, students chose four to include in their final English 1 portfolios. Those course portfolios then served as the basis for a pass/fail evaluation of each student's work at the end of the quarter.

History and Goals of the Portfolio Program

During the ten years prior to implementation of the portfolio program, students at City University were required to pass a timed, impromptu "exit exam" in order to obtain their undergraduate degrees. In the late 1980s, the First-Year English Committee proposed replacing the "exit exam" with a portfolio system, citing a familiar range of shortcomings characteristic of timed, impromptu writing examinations: "the task is decontextualized; students write in a single mode, at a single sitting; their work of three quarters is subordinated to this single 'testing' circumstance" (*Instructor's Guide*, 95). Two years of piloting the portfolio program yielded extensive adjustments and revisions to address concerns for simplicity, fairness, and time constraints, among others. At the end of the piloting period, portfolio assessment was implemented as a required part of all sections of English 1 (*Instructor's Guide*, 2). In the fall quarter during which I conducted my study (in the early 1990s), City University's portfolio program was beginning its second year of full-scale operation.

The primary goal of the portfolio program was the same as for the timed writing test it replaced: to certify to the rest of the university and to the wider world that students who passed the FYE sequence were "proficient" in reading, writing, and critical thinking. Without that certification, students could not complete their undergraduate degrees at City University. Alongside this certification function, instructors and administrators saw the portfolio program as providing important benefits to the teaching and learning of composition at their university, none of which had been offered by the old writing test:

> Students were judged on the basis of their best work
>
> Portfolio assessment supported best practices in the teaching of writing, including invention, drafting, collaboration, research, and revision
>
> Group meetings and discussions (described below) provided a professional community for instructors within which they felt both safe and stimulated to grow as professionals
>
> Involving outside instructors in evaluative decisions enhanced the fairness and impartiality of the judgments, while also boosting program standards
>
> The portfolio program served a public-relations function, demonstrating the seriousness with which writing was taught and assessed in the First-Year English Program.

Structure of the Portfolio Program

The FYE portfolio program consisted of an intricate system of meetings, discussions, and decisions. Figure 1, "Structure of the Portfolio Program at City University," lays out hierarchical and logistical relationships among the fifty individual instructors and three administrators who staffed the program and among the various groups to which they belonged.

Figure 1
Structure of the Portfolio Program at City University

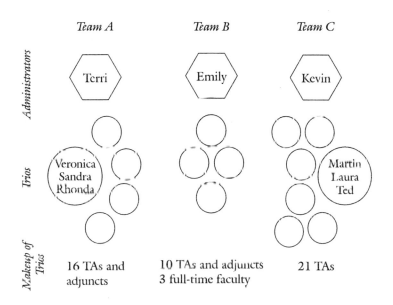

In Figure 1, English 1 faculty are divided vertically into Teams A, B, and C. The administrator leading each team is named in the hexagon at the top of each team. The circles represent instructor-trios, from which I selected two for inclusion in my core group of participants. Names of the instructors in those two core trios, who are quoted extensively in the following chapters, are listed within their respective circles. At the bottom of Figure 1, I provide basic information about the institutional makeup of each team. These figures on numbers of full-time faculty, adjuncts, and TAs do not include the team leaders.

To accommodate different teaching schedules and to limit the size of groups in norming discussions, the twenty-nine experienced English 1 instructors were divided into Teams A and B. Terri, a graduate student in English and assistant to the director of First-Year English, led Team A. Emily, director of First-Year English and a tenured professor, led Team B. The twenty-one teaching assistants (TA's) who made up Team C were all new to teaching English 1 and were all enrolled in the graduate teaching practicum taught by Kevin, associate director of First-Year English and also a tenured professor. Kevin and his practicum students comprised Team C, though Terri led Team C's end-of-term, portfolio norming session because Kevin was unavailable to do so. While Figure 1 provides a static snapshot of institutional relations among program participants, unfolding events in the portfolio program can best be understood in three dimensions: cycles, modes, and roles.

Two cycles: midterm and end-term Over its twelve-week lifespan, the English 1 portfolio program underwent two nearly identical cycles of evaluative deliberations: a midterm cycle and an end-term cycle. What distinguished the two cycles was that at midterm participants judged English 1 students' individual essays. At the end of the term, portfolios made up of four essays each were the objects of evaluation.

Two modes: norming and trio sessions Each cycle (midterm and end-term) featured group discussions in two modes: norming sessions and trio sessions. In norming mode, each of the three teams discussed the four sample texts found in the *Instructor's Guide,* attempted to articulate their "standards" for evaluation, and voted on—and debated—whether and why each sample text should pass or fail. (I strongly encourage readers to study these sample texts for themselves before reading the following chapters. See appendix B, "Selected Sample Texts from City University.") Norming sessions typically lasted two hours. From norming sessions, instructors went forth and met in instructor trios. Trios collaboratively made the "live" decisions to pass or fail all "borderline" students—those whose instructors had judged the student's work to merit a grade of C or below.

Three roles: teacher, outside evaluator, and administrator Because each student's classroom instructor knew the full pedagogical context within which that student composed his or her portfolio, the teacher played an important, sometimes dominant, role in making evaluative decisions in trios. The teacher's fellow English 1 instructors, who shared the teacher's knowledge of the program and the curriculum, played the role of outside evaluators. Precisely because they lacked the teacher's rich knowledge about a particular student, outside evaluators wielded their own distinctive authority in deciding which students passed English 1. Administrators carefully limited their monitoring of and involvement with instructors' trios, but through the norming process they influenced evaluative decisions, based on their extensive knowledge of the history, theory, and scholarship that informed the portfolio program. (For further discussion of these three complementary forms of evaluative authority, see Broad 1997.)

Chronology of Program Events

Table 1, "Chronology of Key Communal Events in City University's Portfolio Program," allows readers to see precisely how the cycles, modes, and roles described above flowed sequentially.

Where I thought additional detail might prove helpful to understanding my analysis, I have provided it below.

Selection and evaluation of sample texts (preceding spring)   In the spring preceding my fieldwork, the three administrators (Emily, Kevin, and Terri) examined essays and portfolios submitted by instructors as prospective sample texts for evaluation and discussion in future norming sessions. Administrators selected four essays (for midterm norming) and four portfolios (for end-term norming) as sample texts with the stated intention of eliciting certain kinds of judgments and provoking discussion of certain issues in norming sessions the following fall. In interviews, administrators explained that they chose essays to represent a range from "excellent" to "poor" writing quality and to raise such issues as "control of language" or "basic technical competency," storytelling ability, depth of critical thinking, and writers' use of nonacademic dialect.

Preparations for midterm norming (week 3)   In preparation for midterm norming, instructors read the four sample essays ("Anguish," "Pops," "Gramma Sally," and "Belle"), decided whether to vote "pass" or "fail" on each essay, and reflected on how they reached their pass/fail decisions. Meanwhile, the three program administrators met in closed session for about half an hour to review their agreed-upon decisions on each text and to share and rehearse arguments in support of those decisions. Administrators also made an effort to anticipate "trouble" in norming discussions, trying to foresee which texts would likely provoke dissent among the instructors, which instructors were most likely to dissent, and what arguments might arise in support of dissenting evaluations. In these ways administrators prepared to "norm" all English 1 instructors to a clear and cohesive sense of program standards that they hoped would lead to "standardized" (that is, quick and consistent) evaluations in trio sessions.

Midterm norming sessions (week 4)   Norming sessions included four phases: preliminary business, voting on sample essays, discussion of sample essays, and wrapping up. One noteworthy characteristic of preliminary business in midterm norming sessions was an opening statement by the

Table 1

Chronology of Key Communal Events in
City University's Portfolio Program

	Chronology		Communal Events
	Preceding Spring		Administrators solicited and selected sample texts for use in next year's norming sessions.
	Weeks 1 and 2		Preliminary program meetings • Administrators welcomed participating instructors • Administrators introduced themselves, distributed and discussed course materials • Group discussed scheduling, policies, and other topics
Midterm Cycle	Norming Mode	Week 3	Preparations for midterm norming • Instructors read sample essays, made pass/fail decisions, and reflected on their evaluative processes • Administrators met to review pass/fail decisions upon which they had previously agreed when selecting sample texts, to rehearse arguments in favor of agreed-upon decisions, and to anticipate arguments from dissenting evaluators
		Week 4	Midterm norming sessions (Teams A, B, and C) • Preliminary business • Voting on sample texts (pass/fail) • Discussion of voting and sample texts • Wrapping up
		Week 5	Preparations for midterm trio meetings • Instructors evaluated all of their own students' writing ("live" texts) • From their students' texts, instructors selected one "A," one "B," and all those judged at "C" or below and brought those selected texts to their trio meetings ("sampling")
	Trio Mode	Week 6	Midterm trio meetings • One "outside instructor" read all of the teacher's C-or-below texts and indicated whether s/he would pass or fail each text • In case of disagreement between a student's teacher and the first outside instructor, the text was passed to the second outside instructor ("third-reader rule") • Trio members discussed, negotiated, and agreed upon a pass/fail decision for each student text read
End-Term Cycle		Week 7	[None]
		Week 8	Preparations for end-term norming (same as for midterm cycle; see Week 3 above)
		Week 9	End-term norming sessions (Teams A, B, and C) (same as for midterm cycle; see Week 4 above)
		Week 10	Preparations for end-term trio meetings (same as for midterm cycle; see Week 5 above)
		Weeks 11 and 12	End-term trio meetings (same as for midterm cycle; see Week 6 above)

leader of the discussion touching upon the purposes, theoretical and historical background, and strategies of "norming." Kevin and Emily delivered such opening statements to their groups; Terri did not.

In each norming session, the administrator-leader wrote the title of each sample text on the chalkboard and then walked the group through the casting and recording of pass/fail votes. On several occasions, instructors resisted administrators' firm directive to "make a [clear] decision" and vote either "pass" or "fail"; some instructors wanted to cast "in-between" votes or to talk about essays before voting on them. Eventually, however, all participants cast a vote one way or the other. Appendix C, "Tabulation of Votes on Sample Texts," displays the votes for the entire program as they were recorded on chalkboards at the end of the various norming sessions and thus indicates levels of consensus and dissent at the end of each norming mode.

The majority of time spent in norming sessions was devoted to discussion of sample texts. At the invitation of the discussion leader, participants volunteered to explain their pass/fail votes. Along with evaluative issues that bore directly upon the decision to pass or fail a particular text, related topics often arose that posed substantial and complex questions or problems for the FYF Program as a whole, such as

> "How do we define 'competency' in English 1?"
> "How important is it for a writer to 'fulfill the assignment'?"

Despite instructors' and administrators' grappling in detail and at length with such pedagogical and evaluative issues in the course of norming discussions, these larger questions were neither addressed nor resolved as decisively as questions about passing and failing particular texts.

End-term cycle (weeks 8 through 12)   As mentioned above, the end-term cycle of norming and trio sessions followed the same pattern as the midterm cycle with one difference: end-term meetings focused upon portfolios of students' writing (four essays including one in-class composition) rather than the single essays discussed and judged at midterm.

This account of my research context begins to answer a central question in qualitative research: "What happened?" To answer the more important ethnographic question "What did it mean?" I employed an array of research methods drawn and adapted from the traditions of qualitative inquiry.

RESEARCH METHODS

Compositionists have begun to explore how teachers and administrators in university writing programs manage the intricacies of shared evaluation (see Allen; Belanoff and Elbow; Reynolds). Still, few studies in the literature of writing assessment systematically analyze communal evaluation as a complex social process, in a specific institutional context, and from multiple points of view within that context. This is the approach I employed to gain insight into what City University's writing instructors really valued in their students' work. The research methods adapted and developed for this study can most usefully be described as an extension of grounded theory (Glaser and Strauss; Strauss and Corbin 1994; Strauss), and, more specifically, as "constructivist grounded theory" (Charmaz). First, I systematically, comprehensively, and recursively analyzed more than seven hundred pages of observational notes, transcripts of group discussions and interviews, and program documents to develop an emic map of City University's terrain of rhetorical values. Working from my best understanding of their experiences, I then brought that conceptual map into dialogue with critiques of traditional writing assessment—and especially of rubrics and scoring guides—current in the literature of evaluation. Extending grounded theory in this way, I found participants' complex criteria for evaluation cast in a new light, suggesting new possibilities for improving communal writing assessment, professional development, and student learning in the classroom. Dynamic Criteria Mapping seizes on those new possibilities.

Background of Research Questions

The good news about the research question driving this study (What did they really value?) is that it did not occur to me until long after my data collection and earlier analyses of those data were complete. From the standpoint of qualitative methods, this late blooming is a good thing because it means this research question could not have inappropriately guided decisions I made in collecting data.

The delayed appearance of questions regarding participants' criteria for evaluating rhetorical performances is also bad news. It means that I did not have the opportunity to interview participants on the most pressing issues in this study, for my interviews were focused on questions appropriate to the analytical frameworks of my earlier research (see Broad 1997; 2000; 1994a; 1994b).

Even though my interview questions focused elsewhere, my interest in new ways to map criteria for evaluation had taken root even before I conducted my City University study. While participating in a variety of communal writing assessment programs during the 1980s and 1990s, I noticed how all judgments were referred back to the scoring guide or rubric. If a criterion did not appear on the rubric, it was discounted as a basis for judging a text; if a criterion did appear on the rubric, it was privileged even if it bore little relevance to the text under scrutiny. This is, of course, exactly how rubrics are intended to work, since their chief purpose is to constrain the range of criteria and thereby boost inter-rater agreement. In these contexts I started to reflect on how rubrics are composed and disseminated as well as how they shape shared evaluation; I began to speculate about what a more detailed, responsive, context-sensitive, accurate account of a writing program's rhetorical universe might look like.

Sometime after my earlier City University inquiries were completed, it dawned on me that this writing program, because it used no scoring guide or rubric, was the ideal setting in which to study criteria for writing assessment in a new way. City University's unconstrained (or, in Diederich's terms, "uncontrolled") evaluation invited instructors to tell unfettered truths about what they valued in the texts before them and compelled others to listen to those truths without dismissing them. In this different atmosphere for communal assessment, participants not only articulated a marvelously rich array of rhetorical values, they also consistently tied their values in shared evaluation settings to their values in first-year composition classrooms. Thus was the analytical approach of this study born, seeking to reveal what instructors really valued in their students' texts.

Establishing and Focusing the Inquiry

In the summer preceding my fieldwork I met with Emily and Kevin (director and associate director, respectively, of the First-Year English Program at City University), and they granted me access to the program for the purposes of my fieldwork. During the program's two preliminary meetings for instructors late in September of that year, I requested the informed, written consent of all participants in the program. All three administrators and forty-eight of fifty instructors granted me their consent to participate. Reservations expressed by two instructors regarding how and whether they wished to participate guided my choices in subsequently narrowing the field of potential participants to a core group.

Defining the core group of participants

As explained above in "Research Context," participants in the FYE portfolio program included fifty instructors of English 1, divided into Teams A, B, and C. During midterm norming (week 4), three factors led me to exclude Team B from the core group of participants:

1. Two members of Team B declined to participate in the research and withheld consent to be recorded or interviewed.
2. Team B had a relatively high proportion of adjunct instructors, several of whom informed me that they simply did not have time to be interviewed.
3. Because of their direct contact with Emily, director of First-Year English, as the leader of their norming sessions, some members of Team B felt certain political risks with particular acuteness.

Once I had limited my main research focus to Teams A and C, I narrowed further my core group of participants by eliminating trios that were incomplete during midterm norming and a trio one of whose members said she didn't have time to be interviewed. Employing what Strauss and Corbin (1998, 201) term "theoretical sampling," I also actively sought out differences in temperament, conduct, and institutional position among the remaining trios. By the end of midterm trio meetings (week 7), this sampling process yielded a core group of four trios—two from Team A and two from Team C—in addition to the three program administrators. Later, during data analysis, I narrowed my core group further, to Trio A-1, Trio C-6, and the three administrators. Quotations presented in my two chapters of findings (chapters 3 and 4) come from these nine individuals in my core group as well as from other members of the norming teams to which my core group belonged.

DATA COLLECTION

I gathered data on the FYE Portfolio Program by observing group meetings, interviewing individual participants, and studying program documents of various kinds. In the actual process of my inquiry, these activities were often juxtaposed, interwoven, and overlapping. To clarify and explicate my methods, this section separates out and details each of these three data-gathering activities.

Observations

I observed and recorded three kinds of group events: norming sessions (six) and trio meetings (fourteen), at both midterm and end-term, and an administrative meeting in preparation for end-term norming. Each time I observed an event, I made two kinds of records: observational notes and audio or video recordings (or both). I recorded observational notes on every behavior that I thought might turn out to be significant to my analysis. Verbatim transcripts from audio and video recordings expanded my analysis beyond what observations and field notes alone would have made possible and enabled me to study important themes from multiple points of view.

Interviews

Through twenty-seven formal, semi-structured interviews and several informal, impromptu interviews with individual participants, I discovered, developed, and tested interpretations of group events and themes of analysis. I began each interview with an open-ended invitation to the interviewee to reflect upon the events of the portfolio program, such as "As you look back on last quarter's portfolio program, what stands out in your mind?" By starting with such "grand tour" (Agar 1980) questions and following up on them, I was able to build each interview around topics and concerns introduced by participants rather than by me, the researcher. Later during the same interviews, and in second and third interviews where possible, I often asked prepared questions on topics that had arisen from my observations and analyses up to that point. I also posed questions about particular passages in transcripts, inviting the interviewee to look over the transcript before answering the question. This process allowed me to get participants' commentaries on and interpretations of the details of previous events to inform and guide my own analyses. Appendix D provides a sample schedule of interview questions. However, because the research questions for this study only emerged later, I did not pose interview questions focused on criteria for evaluation. Fortunately, some useful material emerged from interviews anyway. One prime opportunity for future research would be for a researcher to study a program's values as I did, but also to formulate interview questions asking participants what they meant when they invoked a particular criterion and why those criteria matter to them. Such an interview-focused study would, I expect, provide extremely useful insights beyond what I was able to learn.

Documents

Because documents powerfully shaped events and decisions in the program, they formed another important source of data. Documents collected and analyzed included:

The mission statement for the First-Year English Program,

The program's *Instructor's Guide,* which included the sample papers and portfolios discussed in norming sessions and which guided instructors through the portfolio system,

Drafts and Breezes, a selection of essays from previous years' first-year English students,

The St. Martin's Guide to Writing (Axelrod and Cooper) and *A Writer's Reference* (Hacker), the two official required texts for English 1,

Several current students' portfolios discussed during trio meetings

Course readers (collections of articles from the literature in composition and rhetoric) for the two graduate courses attended by the first-year graduate TAs participating in my study, and

Various memos, forms, and information sheets distributed by administrators to instructors.

In helpful contrast to the hurried, day-to-day decisions and actions squeezed into the ten-week academic quarter during which I made my observations, these written materials revealed some participants' more reflective, more historically and theoretically grounded perspectives on the events of the program. At various times during the quarter, participants also referred explicitly to program documents in advocating particular judgments of specific students' texts. For both these reasons, program documents provided important points of triangulation with my other data.

DATA SELECTION AND ANALYSIS

My analyses of data passed through three overlapping but distinguishable phases. The first phase, *concurrent analysis,* took place during the twelve weeks of on-site fieldwork and involved reading the incoming data to guide me in gathering new data. Phase two covered the first several months of work on the current study and involved *comprehensive analysis* of all transcripts and documents to identify, define, and develop all criteria for evaluation mentioned by my participants. Strauss and Corbin (1998) call this stage of data analysis "open coding," and Guba terms it the "discovery mode." In the final phase, *close analysis and verification* (named after what Guba calls "verification mode" and closely related to Strauss and Corbin's "selective coding"), I tested and refined my Dynamic Criteria Map for City University and other findings (see chapters 3 and 4).

Concurrent Analysis

The events of the twelve-week portfolio program rushed rapidly past all of us—participants and researcher—and then were finished. To keep myself afloat on that stream of events, I conducted concurrent analysis (formulation of interview questions based on recent events in the program) on the basis of field notes, notes from (not transcripts of) tape recordings, and memories of events available to interviewees and to me, the researcher. The first twelve weeks of the study were, therefore, heavier on data collection than on data analysis.

Interviews integrated questions about and reflections on recent events from both participants and the researcher. One example was Kevin's impromptu suggestion that I interview him immediately following Team C's midterm norming session. His conflict with a first-year TA named Ted over the evaluation of the sample essay "Anguish" made Kevin want to talk about that event immediately after it occurred, so we did. (In a later interview I asked Ted his view of this same conflict.) Working from statements recorded verbatim in field notes, I also asked interviewees about their own or others' particular statements or actions.

As I explained above, my interest in studying the criteria by which instructors and administrators at City University judged students' writing emerged long after my earlier analyses of the data I collected. After deciding to conduct a full-scale qualitative inquiry into these evaluative dynamics, I pursued a fresh course of the second and third phases of data analysis.

Comprehensive Analysis

As I began this phase of treating the data, I searched my entire data pool (approximately seven hundred single-spaced pages of transcripts and documents) for every comment or passage in a transcript that would help answer the question "Why did that participant pass or fail this text?" (because she found it "clichéd," for example) Using QSR Nvivo software for computer-assisted qualitative data analysis, I coded every passage mentioning criteria for evaluation, defined as "any factor that an instructor said shaped or influenced the pass/fail decision on a student's text." My initial list of criteria included 124 distinct factors drawn from approximately 18,500 lines of transcripts specifically devoted to discussing one or more criteria.

Charmaz provides a useful summary of the "constant comparative method," which lies at the heart of data analysis as practiced in constructivist grounded theory.

> The constant comparative method of grounded theory means (a) comparing different people (such as their views, situations, actions, accounts, and experiences), (b) comparing data from the same individuals with themselves at different points in time, (c) comparing incident with incident, (d) comparing data with category, and (e) comparing a category with other categories. (515)

Readers of the current study will see evidence throughout my findings of all these comparative activities.

With some vexation I note that comprehensive analysis—which involved literally hundreds of hours of searching, sifting, sorting, and cross-checking—can be aptly summarized in a couple of brief paragraphs. I console myself, however, with calling readers' attention to how intensively qualitative researchers process data in order to generate conceptual insights.

Close Analysis and Verification

The coding and verification process during this final phase of data analysis refined my interpretations in useful ways. I developed my three levels of grouping criteria (evaluative criteria, criteria categories, and constellations) through repeated and close examinations of the data, and I modified categories extensively in response to what I found there. For example, I found that my list of textual criteria fell into two distinct areas: textual qualities and textual features. Textual criteria also dropped from eighty-two to forty-seven in number. This refinement and condensation of criteria took place when I recognized that some criteria from the earlier list needed to be merged to reflect participants' evaluative frameworks as accurately as possible. For example, "Dialogue" was merged with "Detail and Description"; I merged "Tone" into "Style, Concision." References to "comma splices," which I had originally categorized under "Punctuation," turned out upon reflection and research to be actually a part of the criterion "Grammar." Through this process of refinement I met the qualitative researcher's responsibility to encourage the data to "resist" the researcher's presuppositions and expectations (see Agar; Flower; Guba; Miles and Huberman; Patton) by actively pursuing alternative interpretations of events and attempting to account for all data.

Sifting carefully through large coding reports on each criterion, I first developed my understanding of those individual criteria and then discovered many interrelationships among criteria. Repeated passes through the coding reports yielded more and more finely distinguished, richly illustrated, and complexly interrelated understandings of criteria that eventually served as the structure and content for the Dynamic Criteria Map discussed below.

This account of the theoretical bases and qualitative methods I drew upon in collecting and analyzing my data should help my readers to judge the validity, or persuasiveness, of the analyses and conclusions presented below and to succeed when they try Dynamic Criteria Mapping in their own writing programs. What follows is my exploration and mapping of the criteria according to which participants made their pass/fail judgments of students' texts at City University.

3

TEXTUAL CRITERIA
What They Really Valued, Part 1

We can now look at answers to the question: What did instructors and administrators in City University's First-Year English Program value in their students' writing? The multifaceted, surprising findings of this study strongly suggest the depth of self-knowledge and truthfulness of self-representation that other writing programs could gain by conducting Dynamic Criteria Mapping.

Before readers look at my findings, however, I urge them to read the sample texts presented in appendix B, "Selected Sample Texts from City University,"[2] and to make their own notes on the strengths and weaknesses they perceive in these texts. Readers who take time now to read and evaluate these sample texts will not only better understand and appreciate the findings I am about to present, they will experience this exploration of City University's evaluative terrain as "insiders." In addition, readers may find appendix E helpful in understanding the system of abbreviations that I use in referencing excerpts from the transcripts in this and later chapters.

QUALITATIVE AND QUANTITATIVE OVERVIEWS OF CRITERIA FOR JUDGMENT

Before delving into detailed findings from my study of City University's portfolio assessment program, we need to glimpse the big picture. Figure 2 provides a graphical "Overview of Dynamic Criteria Mapping for City University."

Though this figure masks nearly every interesting element of my analyses, it provides a useful visual and conceptual sketch of the three main categories of criteria for evaluation and how they are related. Textual Criteria include those factors (such as "detail" and "texture") inherent in the specific text under evaluation. By contrast, the exact same text might pass or fail depending on which Contextual Criteria participants invoke (for example, what is best for the student-author or what are the goals of the English 1 course).

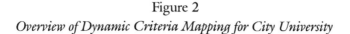

Figure 2

Overview of Dynamic Criteria Mapping for City University

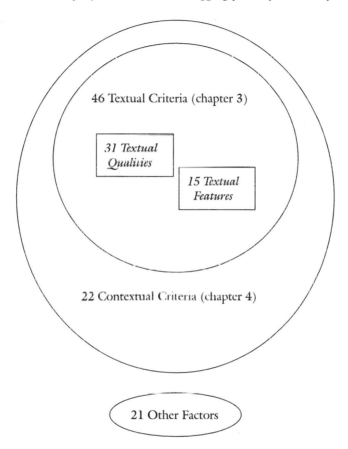

46 Textual Criteria (chapter 3)

31 Textual Qualities

15 Textual Features

22 Contextual Criteria (chapter 4)

21 Other Factors

Textual Criteria fell into two distinct subcategories: Textual Qualities and Textual Features. (The distinction between Qualities and Features is explained below.) Other Factors (neither Textual nor Contextual) also figured into participants' evaluative decisions. This book explores Textual and Contextual Criteria in detail, but does not analyze Other Factors.

Table 2, "Quantitative Analysis of All Criteria for Judgment," provides a numerical overview of all criteria judges invoked when defending and negotiating their evaluative decisions. As with the spatial representation in figure 2, readers who take a few minutes to browse this table will gain a useful overarching grasp of the criteria discussed in this chapter and the next.

As table 2 shows, participants named a total of eighty-nine substantial and distinct kinds of criteria that informed their judgments of students' writing. Those criteria fell into three major categories:

1. Forty-six Textual Criteria (either qualities or features of the text being judged)
2. Twenty-two Contextual Criteria (issues not directly related to the text being judged)
3. Twenty-one Other Factors (additional dynamics shaping evaluative decisions)

Table 2

Quantitative Analysis of All Criteria for Judgment

CATEGORY: **Criterion**	**Transcript lines coded**	**Passages coded**	**Coded in # of transcripts out of 27**	**% (rounded) of transcripts partially coded for this criterion**
TEXTUAL CRITERIA (46 criteria)				
Textual Qualities (aspects of reading experience) (31 criteria)				
Significance/Development/Heart	731	117	18	67
Interesting/Lively/Creative	389	67	18	67
Thinking/Analysis/Ideas	367	60	13	48
Unity/Harmony/Connection	344	55	16	59
Effort/Taking Risks	316	60	19	70
Revision/Process	288	39	11	41
Focus/Pace/Concise	276	49	12	44
Control/Boundaries	221	39	15	56
Style/Tone/Diction/Concision/Dialect	217	28	11	41
Organization/Structure/Flowing/Momentum	214	30	15	56
*				
Empty/Hollow/Clichéd	186	24	13	48
Voice/Personality	170	30	12	44
Mystery Criterion	169	39	10	37
Clarity/Confusion	99	20	10	37
Competent/Knows How To Write	98	17	8	30
Goals/Purposes/Intentions	95	14	5	19
Persuasive/Convincing/Powerful	90	18	11	41
Audience Awareness	76	15	6	22
Sophisticated/Elegant/Mature	58	9	5	19
Tight/Subtle/Minimalist/Show Not Tell	47	8	5	19

*   Empty rows in this table are intended to divide the long lists of criteria into visually and/or mathematically meaningful groups. Usually the breaks come between groups of ten criteria. In the case of several criteria that are broken out into subcriteria, a break comes at the end of the list of subcriteria.

Writer's Attitude	40	8	5	19
Authority/Take Charge/Serious	33	7	5	19
Sincerity/Honesty/Innocence	32	6	4	15
Giving The Teacher What She Wants	31	4	2	7
Humor	29	6	3	11
Consistency/Contradiction	23	5	2	7
Redundancy/Repetition	21	7	3	11
Texture/Richness/Artful	17	5	2	7
Distanced	12	2	2	7
Writing Ability (General)	8	3	3	11
Relevance	7	2	2	7

Textual Features (elements of text)
(15 criteria [counting Mechanics and Sentences as one each])

Mechanics/Conventions/Mistakes/ Errors (not including sub-themes listed below)	901	119	22	81
Grammar	331	69	18	67
Punctuation	159	31	9	33
Spelling	96	23	9	33
Usage	46	13	5	19
Capitalization	14	4	3	11
Typing	14	4	3	11
Legible	8	2	1	4
Format	2	1	1	4
Total for Mechanics/Conventions	1571	266		
Content/Topic	420	63	15	56
Sentences(not including subthemes listed below)	250	54	18	67
Sophistication	44	8	6	22
Variety	42	7	4	15
Clarity	19	4	3	11
Total for Sentences	355	73		
Detail/Description/Examples/ Dialogue	295	50	14	51
Length/Amount (Of Text)	166	22	10	37
Objectionable Views, Characters, and Events	144	16	7	26
Endings/Conclusions	108	18	7	26
Paragraphing	99	20	10	37
Portrayal of Characters and Relationship	43	3	2	7
Leads/Beginnings	31	8	4	15
Transitions	18	4	3	11
Anecdotes	17	2	2	7
Title	10	3	3	11
Messy Appearance	9	1	1	4
Graphics	8	1	1	4

CONTEXTUAL CRITERIA (22 criteria)			
Standards/Expectations	1344	127	23	85
Constructing Writers	725	109	14	52
Fulfilling the Assignment	713	78	15	56
Learning/Progress/Growth	281	37	9	33
Plagiarism/Originality	223	15	7	26
Nature of Pass/Fail Judgment	216	25	11	41
Essay vs. Portfolio	212	22	8	30
Ready for English 2	196	28	10	37
Benefit to Student	132	15	11	41
Nontext Factors	115	14	6	22
Goals for English 1	72	6	4	15
Difficulty of the Writing Task	65	10	4	15
Writing Center	65	11	6	22
Fairness/Hypocrisy	43	4	2	7
Writer Shows Promise	42	8	3	11
Cultural Differences	35	4	2	7
Using the Spell Check	30	2	1	4
Constructing Teachers	16	2	2	7
Compassion for Writer	14	2	2	7
Time	14	3	3	11
Turned in Late	10	1	1	4
Attendance	7	2	2	7
OTHER FACTORS (21 factors)			
Relations (not including subthemes listed below)	8	2	1	4
Teaching and Evaluation	586	58	16	59
Relations among Evaluators	276	29	9	33
Norming and Trios	238	23	7	26
Relations among Texts	214	19	6	22
Relations among Criteria	112	14	9	33
Classroom and World	68	10	6	22
Content and Form	27	3	2	7
Sample Texts and Live Texts	24	2	2	7
Midterm and Endterm	8	1	1	4
Writers' Strengths & Weaknesses	8	1	1	4
Totals for Relations	1561	160		
Borderline/Undecided/Change of Mind(what made it hard to make up your mind?)	1370	179	25	93
Consensus and Dissent (what made it hard to agree?)	1154	92	19	70

Evaluators: Comments About	698	78	20	74
Evaluation Process	379	33	9	33
Program Policies: Revision	269	14	5	19
Comparing Texts	224	21	6	22
In-class Essay	130	5	1	4
Professional Development	84	5	2	7
Evaluating Each Others' Teaching	4	1	1	4
References to Other Events and Texts	3	1	1	4

This chapter will explore findings regarding Textual Criteria, the largest of the three categories. The following chapter discusses Contextual Criteria.

Criteria in table 2 above are ordered according to the number of transcript lines coded for each criterion. Those criteria discussed in the largest number of transcript lines (discussed most often or at the most length) are listed first; those mentioned in the fewest lines (discussed least often or most briefly) are listed last. Though frequency and length of discussion about a particular criterion does not simply equate to its significance or importance in the program (that is a qualitative judgment), quantitative sequencing does provide useful information about relationships among criteria for evaluation.

The quantitative information provided in the other three columns of table 2 can generate additional insight. Comparing the number of transcript lines coded for any criterion to the number of passages coded yields a ratio between how *much* that criterion was discussed and how *often* it was discussed. Some criteria might be discussed relatively few times, but at considerable length, or vice versa. The third column in this table, showing number of transcripts out of twenty-seven in which a criterion was coded, indicates in how many different settings or events that criterion was discussed. In other words, it points to the breadth to which participants found the criterion important enough to mention. The final column in table 2 simply converts the "number of transcripts out of twenty-seven" ratio to a percentage figure for easy assessment of how broadly that criterion was discussed across the norming, trio, and interview transcripts.

Generating a detailed, complex, and accurate list of the criteria by which we judge students' writing is itself a worthy goal, particularly when we compare the richness of this list with the sparse contents of a standard five- or six-category scoring guide (such as "focus, support, organization, conventions, integration," per Illinois Standard Achievement Test of Writing). However, the most important and interesting discoveries of what was really valued at City University are revealed not in table 2 but in the results of my qualitative analyses: the Dynamic Criteria Map. This map illustrates dynamic relations among and within Textual Criteria and offers provocative insights into the acts of teaching and assessing writing.

Textual Criteria

Evaluators at City University articulated two kinds of Textual Criteria for evaluation: Textual Qualities and Textual Features. Both categories were highly important to judgments formed by participants in my study, and both received a great deal of attention in their discussions.

Significance/Development and *Voice/Personality* are two examples of Textual Qualities. These criteria emerge from a judge's sustained intellectual, emotional, and aesthetic engagement with a text. Textual Features, by contrast, can nearly always be physically pointed to: for example, problems with *Mechanics* or the presence of *Dialogue.* Evaluators can also identify Textual Features without entering fully or deeply into the rhetorical and literary experience of a text; some Textual Features (*Length/Amount* or *Paragraphing,* among others) can be assessed without reading a single word of the text being judged. Thus, Textual Features are available to a quick assessment, to a reading oriented to the surface of the text. Since City University's administrators and instructors discussed Textual Qualities somewhat more than they did Textual Features, I begin my discussion of Textual Criteria with the subcategory of Textual Qualities.

TEXTUAL QUALITIES

The map of textual qualities valued at City University includes seven distinct constellations of criteria (plus three constellation-independent criteria). As illustrated in figure 3, "Dynamic Criteria Map of City University's Textual Qualities," I have grouped criteria into seven constellations, each of which I address separately below.

I recommend that readers lay out the large format Dynamic Criteria Map (see pocket inside the back cover) and follow along during the ensuing discussion, moving from one criterion to the next and noting juxtapositions and interconnections among them as they go.

In the following discussion I devote primary emphasis to those criteria that were quantitatively or qualitatively most significant. Unfortunately, space limitations require me to disregard a number of criteria, including several with interesting and worthwhile stories to tell.

Figure 3

Dynamic Criteria Map of City University's Textual Qualities

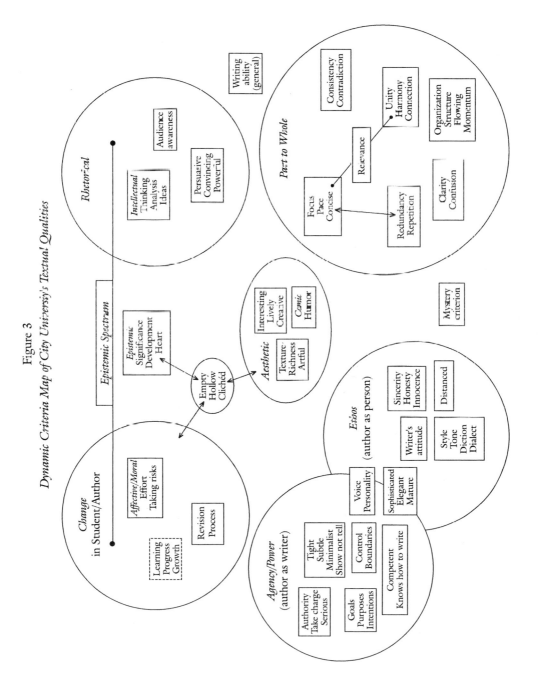

The Epistemic Spectrum

The most substantial criterion of Textual Quality was *Significance/ Development/Heart* (henceforth abbreviated simply as *Significance;* see Figure 4). In vivo synonyms and antonyms for this criterion are listed below.[3] Careful reading of these excerpts will reward readers with a feel not only for the richness of the discourse clustered at each criterion, but also for the personalities and passions of the instructor-evaluators whose writing program I studied.

Significance/Development/Heart

Synonyms: significance, development, fleshed out, elaboration, explo-ration, involved, depth, substance, complexity, meaning, follow-through, extend, accomplish, movement, moving forward, heart, storytelling, thoughtful, reflective, engaged, discover, make knowledge, learning by writ-ing, address (vs. mention), pursues, builds something up, goes somewhere with it, thorough, the unspoken, the other stuff (vs. mechanics)

Antonyms: fly over it; hurried; listing information; just action; skimmed over some material; didn't do much with; didn't cover a lot of [evaluation] criteria . . . just told about what the movie was about and the characters; like a journal entry. It lacks finality . . . just very limited in its content . . . the in-class was a write-off . . . It's a this-then-this; doesn't go anywhere from there; it's dead; doesn't know where to go with it; slight; perfunctory

Significance indicates that the reader experiences something meaning-ful, weighty, important, worthwhile, or affecting during her encounter with the text. *Significance* is an intellectual, emotional, and poetic experi-ence. It is also a close fit with one of the two prime goals laid out in the FYE Program mission statement:

One broad goal [of the program] is to teach students that writing is a way of thinking and that in the very act of writing about a particular subject for a particular audience, the writer will discover new knowledge.

The great prominence of the epistemic criterion *Significance* in the discussions I studied must count as an important success for the FYE Program in reaching this "broad goal" of the program.

Given its preeminent status among criteria of Textual Quality, *Significance* could legitimately be called the heart of what instructors at City University wanted writing to be and do. Instructor-evaluators wanted to see knowledge made in the texts they read, so I termed this

Figure 4
The Epistemic Spectrum

	Epistemic Spectrum	
Affective/Moral	*Epistemic*	*Intellectual*
Effort	Significant	Thinking
Taking risks	Development	Analysis
	Heart	Ideas

value "epistemic." *Significance* is something more than just creative or critical thinking (see *Thinking/Analysis/Ideas*). It is fundamentally about learning-by-writing. For one can think without learning; one can arrange one's arguments in logical and persuasive ways without considering other points of view or changing one's own views. By contrast, *Significance* focuses on the particular, hard-to-define performance by which writers demonstrate that they are learning something by being "engaged" with their material, by "exploring" it, by "discovering" and "elaborating" within their topics, by showing their moral or intellectual "movement" over the course of the text.

Another crucial pedagogical point emerging from my examination of the criterion *Significance/Development/Heart* was that instructors wanted to *find* significance in a text, but they didn't want to be *given* significance. Several comments coded under *Significance* showed evaluators complaining that the significance in the sample essay "Pops" was "tacked on" at the end in an unconvincing way.

> *Peter:* 'Cause the end has that corny, tacked on feeling: "Okay, now's the part where I have to say . . . how important this was. 'Cause it didn't come through in the beginning, right? (A Mid Norm, 489)
>
> ***
>
> *Hal:* I mean it's as if an anecdote has been inserted . . . and uh, and a conclusion is there which then sort of distills the apparent significance.

Students need to know not only that *Significance/Development/Heart* is a prime criterion for evaluation, but also that they must provide that quality by "showing rather than telling" (see the related criterion *Tight/Subtle/Minimalist* in the *Agency/Power* constellation). They must trust their readers to find the significance embedded in their narratives and descriptions and not shove it in their faces.

Significance was closely related to two other criteria, between which it stood as a hybrid. On the one hand, *Significance* was related to—though also, as explained above, distinct from—the intellectual virtues of *Thinking/Analysis/Ideas.* On the other hand, the moral elements of *Significance* as a quality that demonstrates the courage required to explore, engage, and develop a topic linked it with *Effort/Taking Risks.* Arrayed together, these three substantial textual qualities comprise the *Epistemic Spectrum.*

"Change in Student-Author" Constellation

At the *Effort/Taking Risks* end of the *Epistemic Spectrum* lies the *Change in Student-Author* (abbreviated below as *Change*) constellation, made up of three criteria:

> *Learning/Progress/Growth* [4]
> *Effort/Taking Risks*
> *Revision/Process*

The vital, though unsurprising, concept around which the *Change* constellation coheres is that writing instructors wanted to see their students change for the better.

Learning/Progress/Growth often emerged, for example, in discussions of portfolios. Evaluators would comment with satisfaction on the fact that the four pieces in a portfolio showed steady progress on one or more criteria (*Length, Significance,* or *Mechanics,* for example), or they expressed alarm that the pieces in the portfolio "got weaker as [the portfolio] went along."

Effort/Taking Risks distills and amplifies the moral and affective values latent in the *Significance* criterion. These are qualities in texts that led readers to admire the author. When, on the other hand, the qualities of effort and risk taking were perceived as missing, the author might be viewed as a slacker who doesn't care about herself, her writing, or her instructor.

Effort/Taking Risks
Synonyms: effort; work; taking risks; engagement; engaged; ambition; ambitious; struggle; wrestling; choices; aware; attempt; worked really hard; was getting somewhere; [student sought instructor's help]; really trying; done a lot of work; try something harder; tries some difficult things; reaches too high; shows a lot of work, a lot of attention; put some effort into it; the student is working it out

Figure 5
Change in Student-Author

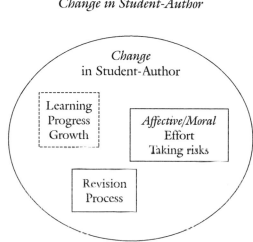

Antonyms: they almost haven't tried; he doesn't really try in there; he doesn't want to deal with some explosive stuff; the student didn't seem to take much trouble with this paper; carelessness; FAILURE to attend to these [errors]; this person did not go and seek help! Did not go and take care of this; I don't see that he put all the effort into this one.

Revision/Process is the first of several criteria to be discussed here that provided explosive challenges to City University's FYE Program, challenges that urgently demanded the program's attention to, reflection on, and negotiation of powerful and competing values. It is worth noting here, however, that because City University lacked a process for recording, negotiating, and publicizing its criteria for evaluation, such opportunities were lost; and issues such as those surrounding *Revision/Process* went unresolved.

A useful start on considering *Revision/Process* as a criterion of Textual Quality is that one might not expect it to appear as a Textual Criterion at all. Since at City University neither essays (at midterm) nor portfolios (at end-term) provided direct evidence of revision or other aspects of writing process and since evaluators were urged by administrators to judge strictly on the basis of the textual evidence that came before them (as opposed to information supplied by the student's instructor), it might have been reasonable to expect *Revision* not to play a significant role in evaluative discourse. On the contrary, however, *Revision* was not only one of the most quantitatively significant criteria, it was also one of the most theoretically and pedagogically instructive.

Various documents in City University's FYE Program made clear that writing processes, especially revision, were important and valuable aspects of the pedagogy of the introductory writing course (English 1) and of the communal writing portfolio assessment system that was an integral part of English 1. The first page of text in the English 1 *Instructor's Guide* quickly established that

> A foremost advantage to students [of portfolio assessment] is that the system allows their best work to be assessed. Essays in their portfolio will be essays that they have labored over, essays that represent the best that they have done in a ten-week writing course. (2)

This advantage of portfolio assessment may have accrued partially thanks to the fact that students omitted one of their first two papers from the final portfolio, but the "best work" benefit also presumably stemmed from the fact that students were allowed and encouraged, within certain constraints, to revise ("labor over") their texts.

The FYE Program "Mission Statement" also provided strong support for teaching and valuing revision:

> Instructors should also be certain that they teach the entire composing process, offering students assistance in prewriting, writing, and rewriting. . . . Rewriting covers revision strategies—adding, deleting, rearranging, and the like—as well as editing skills. (4)

Instructor-evaluators of English 1 responded to such encouragement and direction from administrators by putting significant emphasis on *Revision/Process* in their teaching and evaluation of writing. The following sampling of pro-process excerpts illustrates some of the range of ways in which revision was valued and privileged in the program.

> *Sandra:* His mistake was not getting rid of that when he wrote his final version. (A-1 Mid Trio, 1340)
>
> ***
>
> *Emily:* Also, for the theme that gets written in class, I don't think that you fail this portfolio on the basis of this [unrevised] essay. (Admin Pre-Port Norm, 1017)
>
> ***
>
> *Kevin:* I think this is a very promising paper. And as a first draft, it looks wonderful. I think it needs a lot still. (C Mid Norm, 734)

These remarks suggest that another of the major goals for the FYE Program as a whole was met in the context of English 1: instructors encouraged, required, looked for, and rewarded revision and process as they taught and evaluated. Note how DCM provides rich data for program evaluation as well as in support of student learning and assessment.

Directly alongside the privileging of *Revision/Process* in program documents and in instructors' teaching and assessment of writing, however, stood a powerful and contradictory concept: that *unrevised,* in-class writing provided the "true story" of a writer's ability and was therefore the best guide to whether a student should pass English 1. This position was articulated by Peter and Ben during Team A's End-Term (portfolio) Norming session.

The *Revision* issue arose when Veronica, a graduate-student TA, posed this question to Team A near the outset of their end-term norming session:

I have a question about the in-class paper. . . . I mean how does it actually function in the portfolio, like, does it really help to decide when a portfolio is really "C" or whatever or that it's going to fail. . . . Do you see what I'm asking? I mean, how do we count the in-class essay? (A Mid Norm 1097)

In response to Veronica's query, Peter offered this view privileging the unrevised, composed-in-class text:

It can be a very good determinant of pass/fail. . . . Well, I mean, yeah it's timed writing and everything, but they've also had plenty of time to prepare, and I think just somebody's basic writing skills are more apparent then than who knows how much revision they've done on it, whether it's their roommates'. . .

When Sandra, an adjunct instructor, immediately challenged Peter's antirevision argument, Terri, the norming session leader, supported Peter by reminding Sandra that exam writing goes unrevised, and the in-class essay in the portfolio "is also practice for exam writing." Peter then elaborated on his antiprocess position.

I mean I just think you can tell a lot about the person's ability level from in-class writing, more a lot of times than you can tell from prepared, more worked-over papers where they're thinking "What does my teacher want?" or what's other students' comments on them or something. (A Mid Norm 1134)

For Peter, revision masked a writer's true ability level, whereas unrevised, timed writing revealed it. Ben added this statement in support of Peter's perspective:

I think the in-class is important, because it tells you whether they're ready to move or they're not ready to move. (A Mid Norm 1236)

Discussion on this topic continued for several more minutes, with various instructors exploring and negotiating how in-class writing should be assessed (for example, focus on *Organization* and *Thinking*, and disregard occasional faults in *Mechanics*). Then Team A moved on to discuss other sample texts and other criteria.

This writing program had a serious problem. Its mission statement, its lead administrators, and many of its instructors were privileging *Revision* as a value for judging whether each City University student was capable enough to proceed with his or her degree. Meanwhile, other instructors (and Terri, the assistant to the director of the FYE Program) argued to privilege unrevised over revised writing because unrevised writing was seen as a more reliable indicator of a writer's "true" ability and a test of whether the author may have plagiarized or received undue assistance on the revised texts.

This is precisely the sort of scenario in which the process of Dynamic Criteria Mapping is most helpful. Without a method for placing side by side statements from program documents and candid statements from various norming and trio sessions—some privileging revision and others privileging unrevised prose—a writing program would lack the ability to identify a serious pedagogical and theoretical fissure in the program that is likely to lead to dramatically different pass/fail judgments depending on which of these two "camps" an evaluator has joined. Dynamic Criteria Mapping clarifies the rift, produces a text to illustrate it, and makes it available for programmatic discussion, negotiation, and decision making. Such a process not only helps instructors know how to evaluate and lets students know how they will be evaluated, the process also demonstrates to interested outside parties that the writing program is actively engaged in identifying problem areas of instruction and evaluation and addressing them in a proactive and professional manner.

As noted earlier, *Revision/Process* was highly valued in the program, both in official statements and in the discourse of most instructors. At the same time, in an effort "to protect [instructors] from . . . endless revisions that never stop, that seem to go on forever," the program constrained how much and which essays students were allowed to revise once the instructor had responded to them. Officially, students could revise *only* whichever of their first two essays (important person or significant event) they included in their portfolio. Some instructors accepted this policy limiting revision, while others commented that the policy "doesn't make any sense at all," because

> I just don't feel comfortable saying [to my students] "multiple drafts are the way to do it, except you're not allowed to." (Peter, A Mid Norm 311)

and

> that doesn't make sense to say [to students], "Look at my comments, read every word I say, ponder it—but don't use it." (Florence, A Mid Norm 318)

Instructors handled this tension between limiting workload and encouraging revision by providing their students with varying instructions and levels of freedom regarding which pieces could be revised and how much. Some of those instructors who allowed their students to exceed the official limit experienced an intriguing phenomenon: "revision guilt." Veronica reported that

> I got into trouble in my own classes because I gave them more freedom of choice, I gave them the opportunity to revise a paper that they wanted most to work on as opposed to saying do either [essay number] one or two. (Veronica 1, 702)

***

> Sandra and Rhonda . . . said something about how they don't allow students to revise so how could I have done that. (Veronica 2, 129)

***

> I was reprimanded, do you see what I'm saying? Because of the parameters of the thing. I had this vision of all their students not having this chance to revise and all mine [having that chance]. (Veronica 2, 173)

An interesting side effect of revision guilt was that instructors sometimes coped with it by evaluating their students according to a higher standard. In order to compensate for the unfair advantage they felt they had given their students, they expected less from other instructors' students than from their own. This evaluative dynamic slides into another surprising aspect of revision: that revision was usually viewed as good, but could also be perceived as bad.

In the midterm meeting of Trio A-1, trio-mates Veronica, Sandra, and Rhonda were discussing the hypothetical case of a student "who's done eight drafts to get what they got" and who "came to you [the instructor] every single day [and said] 'What can I do? What can I do?'" I asked these instructors how this hypothetical student's multiple drafts and repeated pleas for direction would affect their evaluation of his work.

Rhonda replied that "it would definitely work in his favor," and Sandra explained that

> The emotional impact—If someone is really, really trying . . . I would hate to say, "Yeah, you're not passing," you know, to someone who has been working really hard.

This comment helps illustrate the strong link between *Revision/Process* and *Effort/Taking Risks* as criteria for evaluation. Veronica, however, offered an answer quite different from her trio-mates':

> Sometimes it might work negatively, too, because if you point out all the sentence-level errors and . . . then the next paper has the same errors, you know, they almost haven't tried. So, the same thing could work negatively.

The same behavior that looks to Sandra and Rhonda like *Effort* and *Revision* could finally register with Veronica as *lack* of effort—"they almost haven't tried." Students should therefore know that multiple drafts and visits to the instructor are not enough to earn credit for *Revision/Process:* they need to undertake the recommended revisions with demonstrated seriousness of purpose.

Furthermore, students can't merely follow the instructor's directions for revision; they need to show independence of judgment and craft. For example, Veronica observed that one student-author

> has a jillion comma splices, which he just mechanically fixed because I marked them. . . . He had them before, too. So, I mean, I was going to fail him, you know.

Veronica demanded that her students do more than "mechanically fix" errors she marked for them. (See the related criteria *Authority* and *Giving the Teacher What She Wants.*) She also doesn't want her students to wait until the last minute to do their revisions.

> He's revised every paper in here. He's just this guy, this person that didn't work for nine weeks, and you know, bellyache a lot the whole time, and then at the end in two days, he's worked this all out.

In this case, though the student had "revised every paper," those revisions did not count in his favor because he waited until the last two days to do them. This is an example of instructors penalizing revision. Here again, students should know that revision can actually count against them if their instructors perceive them as idlers who bail themselves out in the final hour of the course.

Figure 6
Empty, Hollow, Clichéd

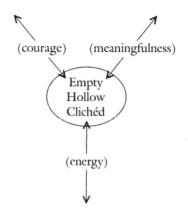

Empty/Hollow/Clichéd

Empty/Hollow/Clichéd

empty, hollow, clichéd, flat, corny, bland, superficial, one-dimensional, boring, nothing wrong with it, abstraction, shell, safe, vapid, formulaic

This criterion cluster is distinctive in two ways. First, it is one of only four criteria in the DCM of exclusively negative quality (the others are Textual Features *Objectionable Views, Characters, and Events* and *Messy Appearance* and the Contextual Criterion *Turned in Late*). Second, it acts as a foil for three other substantial criteria of textual quality: *Effort/Taking Risks; Significance;* and *Interesting/Lively/Creative*. In participants' comments, and thus on the DCM, *Empty/Hollow/Clichéd* was opposed to all three of those criteria.

Empty counterposes *Significance* on the axis of meaningfulness. It opposes *Effort/Taking Risks* on the axis of courage. And it contrasts *Interesting/Lively/Creative* on the axis of energy. For example, those instructors most critical of the sample essay "Pops" called it most of the names listed in the box above. This was in contrast with the sample text "Gramma Sally," which was generally judged strong on all three of the criteria to which *Empty* is opposed, though the essay suffered from many weaknesses of *Mechanics* and *Style*.

Because this is a negative criterion that exists chiefly as the opposite to three other important affirmative criteria for judging students' writing, the data on *Empty/Hollow/Clichéd* offer less basis for commentary than I found for the other criteria discussed here.

The "Aesthetic" Constellation

The three criteria clustered in the *Aesthetic* constellation—*Interesting/ Lively/Creative; Textured/Rich/Artful;* and *Humor*—all provide aesthetic pleasure and satisfaction to readers. (See Figure 7.)

Interesting/Lively/Creative is by far the most quantitatively substantial of the three,

Interesting/Lively/Creative

Synonyms: interesting, fascinating, exciting, creative, innovative, lively, complex, energy, spirit, life, lively, flair, striking, original, out of the ordinary, endearing, appealing, neat, cute, sweet, kept my attention, you wanted to read on, shocking, stunning, surprising, spice, spicy, enjoy, arrest the reader, alive, engaging, inviting, unique, remembered it fondly, vivid, vital, vitality, fresh, something different

Antonyms: conservative; boring ("bored spitless"); abstraction; awful, generalized rambling; unremarkable; flatly competent; pat; didn't turn me on; uninspired

Instructor-evaluators and administrators were unanimous in proclaiming the sample text "Gramma Sally" as a highly *Interesting* essay.

Fred: The dog, I mean . . . It was something out of the ordinary, like, God, this is really interesting. . . . I could see how people would fail it, and it probably should be failed, but I just thought the subject matter was so endearing . . . I didn't want to fail it. I didn't want to. (A Mid Norm, 1091)

***

Kevin: You wanted to read on, to find out. And also, the way she, the woman was torturing the dog . . . was so shocking to me, you know? Kind of sadistic? It was interesting. (C Mid Norm, 413)

***

Kevin: I think this is in some ways the most interesting paper in the group. It's rich with detail, it's full of good examples, it's lively, it's interesting. The writer is clearly deeply engaged in the topic. (C Mid Norm, 908)

The unusually high level of interest, the "lively" and "endearing" qualities of "Gramma Sally" help to explain why FYE Program instructor-evaluators split almost exactly evenly (twenty-four to pass, twenty-six to fail) when it came time to vote on whether the essay met program standards, even when the essay also suffered from serious deficiencies in the areas of *Mechanics, Focus,* and *Style.* The sample text "Pops" was generally

Figure 7
Aesthetic Constellation

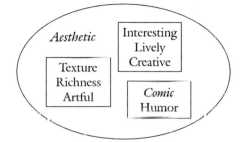

viewed as the mirror image of "Gramma Sally": highly competent at the
level of *Mechanics, Sentences,* and *Style,* it was also judged to be abstract,
pat, and unremarkable. Forty-five instructors voted to pass "Pops," while
six voted to fail it.

An important perspective on the *Interesting* criterion comes from
Grant Wiggins, who complains in several of his publications that he
encounters great difficulty trying to persuade groups of English instructors to place *Interesting* on their rubrics and scoring guides.

> [O]ur skittishness in assessing such things [as "enticingness"] is revealing
> and ironic. Surely . . . these are the kinds of effects we should be scoring. For,
> at its heart, the act of formal writing is designed to move a reader in some
> way. (132–33)

In light of Wiggins's repeated struggles and protests, I take it as a
major point in favor of both the City University FYE Program and of
Dynamic Criteria Mapping that *Interesting/Lively/Creative* not only made
it onto the City University Map, but took a prominent place there.
These are some of the benefits of researching what we really value when
teaching and reading rhetoric, as opposed to placing in a rubric only
what we think we are supposed to value (typically "objective" and "formal" features) in large-scale assessment settings.

The "Agency/Power" Constellation

The *Agency/Power* constellation contains a collection of criteria by
which evaluators constructed a picture of the student-author's characteristics and capabilities as a writer. (See Figure 8.)

Figure 8
Agency/Power Constellation

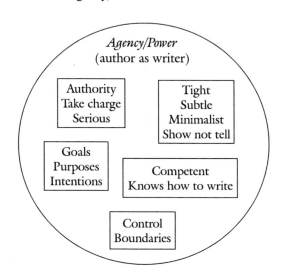

Tight/Subtle/Minimalist/Show-Not-Tell. In the earlier discussion of *Significance,* I noted how instructors wanted to find significance but did not want to be handed significance or hit over the head with it. In a related evaluative dynamic, the criterion *Tight/Subtle/Minimalist/Show-Not-Tell* focuses intensely on the writer's ability to create the textual conditions within which a good reader will find fulfillment without spoiling the experience by overwriting.

Tight/Subtle/Minimalist/Show Not-Tell
   Synonyms: subtle; minimalist; tight, deft suggestions rather than elaborations; she's resting a lot on the things . . . she leaves out; stripped-down style; suggests; understatement; constraint; getting the job done; it shows and it doesn't tell
   Antonyms: overblown; very flowery; belabor its point

Emily, director of the FYE Program, admitted that she had a special appreciation and enthusiasm for the sample essay "Pops," based in her identification with the writer's style:

Probably my own stylistic taste is for minimalist stuff, for tight, deft suggestions rather than elaborations. So in my view, that paper, "Pops", is a very sophisticated, skillful paper. (Emily 1, 45)
                              ***

I was raised reading writers who learned from Hemingway and E.B. White, and so I have a particular, you know, affinity for a certain kind of stripped-down style. So I think I'm a more responsive reader to this style of this paper than I might be to some other papers. . . . It shows and it doesn't tell, it doesn't belabor its point but it suggests it. I like that. I think that's really good. And those are things that I very much value in writing. (Emily 2, 295)

It is interesting to note that some of the passages that instructor-evaluators in the program marked as "clichéd," Emily interpreted and valued as "understated." The fact that one reader's *Cliché* can be another's *Subtlety* suggests that a writing program's Dynamic Criteria Map might contain potentially hidden links among criteria depending on different readers' literary or stylistic orientations.

Goals/Purposes/Intentions and Authority. Two closely related criteria in the *Agency/Power* constellation are *Goals/Purposes/Intentions* and *Authority/ Take Charge/Serious.*

Goals/Purposes/Intentions

Synonyms: purpose; rhetorical purpose; attempting to fulfill a particular purpose; intent; it starts and goes somewhere and does what it ought to do; she's fairly consistent in fulfilling the goals; she was aware of her goals; the essay's goals are fulfilled; the tone and purpose of the essay were in complete harmony; she meant to do it this way; some sense of what they are going to accomplish

Antonyms: he didn't have a sense of what he was trying to do in that paper, where he wanted to go and stuff like that; the effect is just unintentional; it wasn't intended to be what it turned out to be

What we learn from studying *Goals/Purposes/Intentions* is that evaluators noted with appreciation when a writer appeared to know what she wanted to accomplish in a text and furthermore succeeded in accomplishing it. At the same time, those familiar with the history of literary interpretation and criticism may sympathize with the astonished protest from Ted, a graduate TA-instructor on Team C, that tracing (or inventing) authorial intention is a widely discredited method for establishing the meaning and value of a text.

In discussing the sample essay "Anguish" during midterm norming, Team C fiercely debated whether some of the "fractured literary effect" for which some instructors were praising the essay was intentional or a coincidental result of the writer's lack of ability to control language and express thought. Ted exclaimed,

> I'm amazed that people are coming up with this authorial intent kind of stuff. I mean, we're supposed to get that trained out of us [in graduate studies]. We have something here in front of us, let's work on it. (C Mid Norm, 1100)

Ted's colleague Kent responded with the trenchant observation that Ted's praise for the essay's literary effect also relied on a construction of authorial intention, though Kent rephrased Ted's position in dismissive language.

> Well, aren't you saying that she meant to do it this way? That her intent was to come across like she can't write? (1121)

Together, Kent and Ted raised a provocative question for writing assessment: in what ways does and should construction of authorial intentions or goals shape our evaluations?

Authority/Take Charge/Serious. Because references to this criterion often occurred in the same breath as mention of the *Goals* criterion, at one point in my analysis I considered merging the two criteria. They remain separate in the DCM because while *Goals* concerns the writer knowing her rhetorical goals and fulfilling them, *Authority* captures a broader sense of the author's intellectual and rhetorical power. Consideration of the criterion *Authority* also leads us to the two criteria that link and bridge the *Agency/Power* constellation to the *Ethos* constellation: *Voice/Personality* and *Sophisticated/Elegant.*

Authority/Take Charge/Serious

Synonyms: the kind of serious persona we want writers to have; authority; direct; confidence

Antonyms: doesn't take charge of his own writing

The "Ethos" Constellation

The two most closely related constellations on the DCM are *Agency/Power* and *Ethos.* The full map shows these constellations overlapping because both mark evaluators' perceptions of the student-author. *Agency/Power* focuses on the author as a writer; in judging *Ethos,* on the other hand, evaluators respond to their perceptions of the author as a person. In Lester Faigley's terms, City University's writing teachers were as much or more interested in *whom* they want their students to be as in *what* they want their students to write. (1992, 113)

Voice/Personality and *Sophisticated/Elegant* emerge from the distinction and connection between the *Agency/Power* constellation (a judgment of the author's qualities as a writer) and the *Ethos* constellation (a judgment of the author's qualities as a person). It is important to understand how they emerge from and bridge the two constellations.

Voice/Personality

voice; individual; personality; feelings; sense of themselves as a writer; charm; the emotion of her story; emotional; a scream [of "Anguish"]; powerful piece of writing; working with her feelings, clouded by emotion; strong emotional confusion; like seeing her naked; a very mature voice; shifting voice; confidence in [author's voice]; personal

The fact that I could not clearly divide comments related to *Voice/Personality* into synonyms and antonyms points up evaluators' deep ambivalence about many instances of this textual quality. The sample essay "Anguish" provides the most dramatic example of this ambivalence. The raw emotion it presented impressed some readers as courageous, sincere, and honest, but made others uncomfortable ("like seeing her naked") and often led them to judge the writer as not in control of her subject matter or expression. The nuances of these conflicting responses to the *Voice* and *Personality* in "Anguish" help illuminate how this criterion bridges considerations of an author's personal qualities *(Ethos)* and her rhetorical power *(Authority)*. The same is true of the blend of considerations discussed under *Sophisticated/Elegant/Mature*.

Sophisticated/Elegant/Mature

Synonyms: sophisticated, getting a sense of what an essay is; skillful; a very mature voice

Antonyms: inelegant; awkwardness; very beginning writing; mechanical; immature

Here again we find judgments based on qualities that are as attributable to the author's self (mature/immature, sophisticated/inelegant) as to her capabilities as a writer.

Now on to those criteria wholly and firmly located in the *Ethos* constellation.

Figure 9
Ethos Constellation

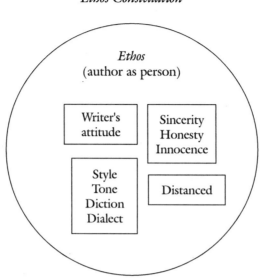

Writer's Attitude might be judged "egocentric, arrogant, humble, or inter-ested" (as distinct from *Interesting*). These perceptions of the author strongly influenced readers' pass/fail judgments. Similarly, if an author was perceived as *Distanced* from her subject and providing *Perspective,* she was generally lauded for it. However, the major debate over the sample essay "Anguish" raised questions about whether authors should be pun-ished for providing "fire" and "splatter" in their essays when the assign-ment and other FYE Program documents encouraged "intensely personal" writing. *Sincerity/Honesty* was a related criterion by which the author was judged truthful and earnest. Faigley discusses this criterion at length in "Judging Writing, Judging Selves" (1989). But the largest crite-rion within *Ethos*—and the point of judgment that will lead us out of the personalness of this constellation and into the more comfortable and familiar ground of clearly rhetorical judgments—is the next one.

Style/Tone/Diction/Dialect focuses on how the author uses language at the word and sentence level, but it excludes the closely related Textual Features of *Grammar* and *Usage,* for example. To illustrate the usefulness and fineness of some of these distinctions, let us consider the concern articulated under the criterion *Style* for apparently unjustified shifts in verb tenses: "moving from the present to the past tense without clear reasons." Verb tense is an issue also treated under *Mechanics: Grammar.* To justify the distinction we must notice that verb tense switching within a sentence is a grammatical problem, whereas verb tense switching between or among sentences is a stylistic problem.

Style/Tone/Diction/Dialect

Synonyms: I liked her style of writing; I think she's a good writer; "Plethora"? Did you teach him that word? That's an awfully big word for this age; articulate; able to move the language around; used sentence fragments dramatically; language control; stripped-down style; outward or topical control of language

Antonyms: a lot of use of the second person, when, really he didn't need to be doing that; extremely wordy; missing words; confusion in her tenses, moving from the present to the past tense without clear reasons; inappropriate tone; dialect interference; lingo; it was the dialect of the student; issues of dialect, issues of non-standard English; a very flowery paper; fluid, extreme, out of control style; language problems

Concerns like diction, concision, missing words, pronoun and verb tense instability among sentences, and dialect belong here under *Ethos* because they are aspects of style and language that lie extremely close to readers' questions about what sort of person the author is. Other language issues more firmly rooted in the author's text make up the criteria that populate the *Part-to-Whole* constellation.

The "Part-to-Whole" Constellation

As the name for this last constellation suggests, criteria positioned here treat the question of relationships among different parts of a text, as well as the relation of a text's parts to the text as a whole. The two most substantial of these criteria are *Unity/Harmony/Connection* and *Focus/ Pace/Concise;* these two criteria also have an intricate interrelationship.

Unity/Harmony/Connection

Synonyms: cohesion, cohesive; coherence, coherent; connection; harmony; unity, unified; mesh together; whole essay works as a unit; rhetorically working together; work together really well; work well within itself; put together in a sensible way; how to put an essay together; [fulfill expectations you create in your readers; don't introduce things you haven't led your reader to expect]; stay with one idea; integrated; correlation; pattern or design; framework

Figure 10
Part-to-Whole Constellation

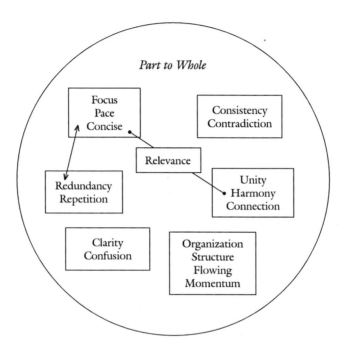

Antonyms: [student's field notes] not really incorporated into the text, it's just sort of stuck there; it doesn't quite all fit together; he didn't go back to the introduction; I would pass half the paper and not pass the other half of the paper; the paragraphs don't work together as an essay; that paper fell apart; not being able to put things together; convoluted and unconnected; it jumps around; thoughts don't seem connected; several different ideas thrown together; disjointed; just didn't seem to go together; incoherent; things falling apart here; falls apart; brokenness; parts don't have any connection to each other; details don't mesh together

Unity/Harmony, as the above excerpts illustrate, concerns how successfully the parts of a student's text work together, a fairly straightforward and familiar criterion for rhetorical judgment. *Unity/Harmony* is the part-to-whole criterion par excellence, with a focus on smooth and satisfying interrelationships among a text's sections. The double-edged criterion *Consistency/Contradiction* is closely related to *Unity/Harmony,* but it focuses on logical rather than on part-to-whole concerns. For example, the author of "Gramma Sally" opened herself up to criticism for inconsistency by reporting an unexpected, hard-to-explain softening toward the title character at the end of her essay. *Consistency* is therefore a logical version of *Harmony*. When texts *Contradict* themselves, by contrast, they demonstrate internal logical disharmony.

Focus/Pace/Concise

Synonyms: focus; pace; pacing; concentrate; she followed it; making the point; limited [scope]; subject gets . . . narrowed in on; stick with something; frame (around it); tight framework; to the point; stayed within boundaries; concise; finding a center to this narrative; sticks to [it]; constraint; getting the job done; worked within [a framework]

Antonyms: [no] high point; totally out of the blue; took such a long time getting started; [not writing about what you lead your readers to expect your text will be about]; he lost track; he lost the topic; rambled/rambling; it's such a large problem [scope]; wordy; paragraphs jump around; jerky; doesn't stay with one idea; cover[s] too much ground; kinda drifts away; drifting; shifting; moved around; long, convoluted; she just rolls and rolls and rolls; belabors the point; go on and on and on; goes off onto a tangent; distracted; tried to bite off everything; long, convoluted . . . could have been stated in a couple of simple sentences

Focus/Pace/Concise is illustrated by counter-example in *Redundancy/ Repetition*, a negative criterion. Material that is repetitive or redundant exhibits faults of *Concision* and *Pace*.

Though they present an unusually large number of synonyms and antonyms, both these criteria (*Unity/Harmony* and *Focus/Pace/Concise*) may be usefully summarized in a single word: "wholeness." Yet they must be distinguished because they address two different kinds of wholeness. *Unity/Harmony* addresses whether and how well all the parts of a text fit with each other. *Focus/Pace*, by contrast, deals with the whole text being about one thing. *Focus* concerns an abstract or overarching wholeness, a wholeness that comes from the relation of the text (in all its parts) to a theme or idea; *Unity* is a relational wholeness, a wholeness that comes from the relations of parts to one another.

As I struggled to understand the relationship between *Focus* and *Unity*, a metaphor suggested itself. Imagine a ship on a journey. The crew and passengers have two kinds of concerns about their ship. First, is the ship strong, solid, and consistently well fitted? This consideration parallels *Unity*. Second, is their ship on course, is it consistently headed toward their destination, is it making good time? These questions pertain to

Focus and *Pace*. The most successful ships, and texts, both hold together and stay on a steady course.

One interesting additional facet of the interrelationships between *Focus* and *Unity* is that *Relevance* is a criterion that applies to both, for material in an essay that lacks relevance can be either off the topic (lacking *Focus*) or not a good fit with other sections of the composition with which it is juxtaposed (lack of *Harmony* and *Coherence*).

Clarity/Confusion. Though my study of the coding report for *Clarity/Confusion* yielded no dynamics worthy of elaboration (in other words, the criterion speaks for itself), it carried illustrative synonyms and antonyms that I thought would prove useful and interesting to students and teachers of writing.

Clarity/Confusion

Synonyms: clarity; clear; clearly explained; makes sense; get your point across; doesn't lose himself in various things; understandable

Antonyms: things are glumphed together; confused; confusing and troubling; unclear; I had no idea what they were getting at; I couldn't understand it!; she kind of lost me; muddy; inconsistent; parts that weren't understandable

Organization/Structure/Flowing/Momentum was likewise self-evident.

Organization/Structure/Flowing/Momentum

Synonyms: organization; structure; order [logical sequence vs. tidiness]; sequence of events; she followed it spatially and temporally; a series of things he's thought about here that he is proposing in some sort of systematic way; its organization makes sense; sticks to that structure absolutely; clear understanding of cause and effect, of . . . how to put an essay together; it did have a beginning and ending and flowed more coherently; arranged differently; transitions jumped from one place to another

Antonyms: he doesn't follow [the argument he set up]; disorganized; structural problems; it didn't follow

Like *Focus*, *Organization* is about staying on track. But whereas *Focus* consists in staying on track in relation to an overarching theme or idea (heading toward the destination), *Organization* concerns a specifically logical movement from one part of the journey to another. In this way, *Organization* is something of a hybrid of *Focus* and *Unity*. *Organization* is *Unity* in motion, *Focus* over time.

Our tour through the Dynamic Criteria Map of City University's Textual Qualities reveals many subtle and complex nuances of evaluation in the writing program, including surprising links and interconnections among those criteria. Examined in the next section of this chapter on Textual Criteria, Textual Features present somewhat less resonant and complex interrelationships than those among Textual Qualities. Nevertheless, Textual Features are important and interesting criteria for evaluation of writing that reward careful study.

TEXTUAL FEATURES

Whereas evaluators' assessment of Textual Qualities (discussed in the preceding section of this chapter) emerged gradually from a deep and sustained engagement with a piece of writing, Textual Features are those aspects of a text that can be recognized—and evaluated—at a glance. For example, instructor-evaluators sometimes criticized texts that came before them for having one or more excessively long paragraphs or, more simply, faulted texts for being altogether too short. It is worth noticing that these two Textual Features, *Paragraphing* and *Length/Amount,* could be—and sometimes were, in fact—adequately assessed by judges who had literally not (yet) read a single word of the text before them.

Also unlike Textual Qualities, the names of Textual Features usually do not inherently convey whether presence of the feature in a text will count for or against the writer. In fact, Textual Features and Textual Qualities often exhibit what might be called a syntactical relationship. Textual Features function like nouns: they identify parts or elements of a text. Textual Qualities function like adjectives: they describe traits experienced when reading. Therefore, it was common to encounter statements from participants in my study that combined the two kinds of Textual Criteria: "What a *boring title.*" (Adjective, noun; quality, feature.) "Her *transitions* were really *elegant.*" (Noun, adjective; feature, quality.) Textual Features are therefore distinct from the Textual Qualities discussed above in how they are perceived, named, and valued.

My study of Textual Features did not yield the same rich network of interconnections as did my study of Textual Qualities. As a result, Textual Features are most effectively presented in the form of a list rather than a map. In order of quantity of discourse devoted to each Feature, table 3 lists the Textual Features discussed in City University's FYE Program.

Table 3
City University's Textual Features

Mechanics
Grammar
Punctuation
Spelling
Usage
Capitalization
Typing
Legible
Format
Content/Topic
Sentences
Variety
Sophistication
Clarity
Detail/Description/Examples/Dialogue
Length/Amount (of Text)
Objectionable Views, Characters, Events
Endings/Conclusions
Paragraphing
Portrayal of Characters and Relationship
Leads/Beginnings
Transitions
Anecdotes
Title
Messy Appearance
Graphics

Mechanics

For several reasons, the clear dominance in City University's evaluative discourse of the Feature *Mechanics* (including its eight subcriteria) merits discussion. First, this Textual Feature demonstrated quantitative supremacy not only over all other Textual Criteria (both Qualities and Features) but also over all other single criteria of any kind (including Contextual Criteria and Other Factors). Yet neither program documents nor comments by the various instructors and administrators in the program indicated that they valued *Mechanics* above all else. Instead, *Mechanics* (more precisely "technical conventions of the dominant dialect") was articulated as one important rhetorical value *among many important others* at the level of the entire FYE Program and in documents about English 1 in particular.

> The First-Year English sequence . . . is about textuality, how texts are produced and consumed; the sequence, therefore, is necessarily about critical thinking, critical reading, and critical writing. (*Mission Statement,* 1)

***

English 1 is a course in writing about personal experience. . . . Instructors should be certain that students understand the effects that the rhetorical context ("the writer's role," "subject matter," "audience," and "purpose") has on the choices that a writer makes. . . . Instructors should also be certain that they teach the entire composing process, offering students assistance in prewriting, writing, and rewriting. . . . An important part of English 1 is ensuring that students understand that it is as "product" that the work of any writer is judged; students should, therefore, learn to edit their work for the grammar, punctuation, and usage that are appropriate to formal writing. Toward this end, students must be familiar with a number of grammatical terms and have a working knowledge of a number of grammatical rules. . . . It is also important to teach a sentence unit (*Mission Statement*, 4)

Explicitly and implicitly, these program documents clearly state that *Mechanics* count. A key question for City University's FYE Program and for this study is: "How did *Mechanics* come to count above *all* other criteria (*Thinking, Significance, Sentences, Authority, Voice, Style, Focus,* and *Organization,* to name just a few) for evaluating students' writing?"

A few participants in my study offered their theories on why, and in what circumstances, *Mechanics* dominated their portfolio evaluation process. Martin, a graduate TA on Team C, offered the most intriguing of these theories. In interviews, Martin explained that he believed members of Team C performed for one another a ritual display of "rigor" focused on *Mechanics.* Martin believed this performance was designed to gain status and respect among their TA peers, as well as from Kevin, their course professor, team leader, and associate director of the FYE Program. (Martin's theory is discussed in more detail in chapter 4, under *Standards/Expectations.*) Rhonda, an adjunct instructor, had a slightly different explanation for the disproportionate emphasis in the program's evaluative discourse on *Mechanics:*

Having things like specific organizational or mechanical things to talk about is a way to equalize everybody, to get rid of the personal contact and defensiveness or whatever, because it's more something that you can point to. "Well, there's a sentence fragment," or something like that. So it's safer ground than other things. (Rhonda, 528)

Perhaps, as Rhonda suggested, *Mechanics* were "safer" to talk about than other, more complex, potentially more contentious aspects of rhetoric.

Or, if Martin is right, focusing on *Mechanics* would earn you status points in the program. Whatever the reasons, this Textual Feature overshadowed all other concerns in terms of the sheer number of lines of transcripts participants devoted to discussing it.

And the dominance of *Mechanics* in the Program was not merely quantitative. Especially in debates during midterm norming on passing and failing the sample texts "Gramma Sally" and "Pops," we can see that mechanics also enjoyed a qualitative superiority or privilege. This Textual Feature came to be seen and used as the "bottom line" criterion for judgment. *Mechanics* as the "bottom line" meant that even though "Gramma Sally" showed tremendous *Significance* and was highly *Interesting* and *Powerful,* because it suffered from many mechanical problems, it therefore failed. On the other hand, even though "Pops" was described by some as "vapid, clichéd, and hollow," it passed because it commanded *Mechanics* quite successfully.

Well more than half the discussion of *Mechanics* as a criterion for evaluation referred to such generalized considerations as "error, editing, mistakes, conventions, competence" without referring to any particular aspect of mechanics that would identify the concern as one or more of the eight specific mechanical concerns listed under *Mechanics.* For example, in urging everyone in Team A to pass the sample essay "Pops" (two instructors had voted to fail it), Terri made this argument:

> We also have to look at the level of writing itse[lf]—you know, is this person making errors? Do they know conventions? Certainly they do, you know? I mean this person is facile in the normal conventions. So I would be hard pressed to fail them just, you know, on that ground. (A Mid Norm, 596)

When, like "Pops," an essay commands conventions with solid (though by no means complete) success, we should not be surprised if evaluators don't pick out specific conventions as examples of that success. Still, for more than half of the extensive discussion of *Mechanics* to omit any reference to specific conventions seems odd. And even when critiquing essays and portfolios with a primary focus on faults in conventions, sometimes participants' comments were still entirely free of references to specific errors or even categories of errors.

> It seems to me that this student for one thing has kind of a proofreading type of problem? You know? The one essay, I forget which one, had tons and tons of mechanical errors. (Peter, A Port Norm, 958)

***

Well, you know, looking at the first essay in this batch, I think that if it were clean, I would have passed [the portfolio]. (C Port Norm, 2008–9)

Particularly in light of the surprising fluidity and porousness of what errors evaluators noticed and identified, what they called them, and how they judged them, the strong predominance of "generic" references to *Mechanics* merits discussion in the program.

The mysteries of *Mechanics* at City University should remind us of Joseph Williams's "The Phenomenology of Error," in which perceptions and judgments of error are subject to what Williams calls "deep psychic forces" (Williams 1981 153).

> Well, it is all very puzzling: Great variation in our definition of error, great variation in our emotional investment in defining and condeming [*sic*] error, great variation in the perceived seriousness of individual errors. The categories of error all seem like they should be yes-no, but the feelings associated with the categories seem much more complex. (155)

As part of some future effort at Dynamic Criteria Mapping, some bold researcher will interview instructor-evaluators regarding the psychodynamics of *Mechanics* (or what James Sosnoski calls the "psycho-politics of error") and bring to light answers to what must remain in my study merely provocative questions.

"Qualifying" Features

With the notable exception of the feature *Mechanics,* most Textual Features were "qualified" when invoked by participants in my study. That is, evaluators worked hard to avoid judging texts by features alone. Instead, they most often spoke of how Textual Features alone could be misleading indicators of the rhetorical success of a text. Perhaps the most dramatic illustration of this intriguing dynamic arises in the criterion *Length/Amount (of Text).*

Length/Amount (of Text). The criterion *Length/Amount (of Text)* included this substantial group of synonyms and antonyms:

Length/Amount (of Text)

Synonyms: [this writer] seems somewhat prolific; she generates a lot; she's got a lot to say; there's a lot more material . . . the person is really engaged in this topic; especially for the in-class paper, I don't think [length] is quite as crucial; she managed, what, a page and a half or something? It's as if she kind of lost her energy after those first two papers; like a student who writes a lot but then in the end, well . . . ; wow, what a long in-class paper . . . All in forty-five minutes?; every single thing that I read of hers seemed hurried, even though some of them are like four or five pages; she writes an abundance, but a lot of what she's putting in there seemed totally irrelevant to me to what she was saying; it just got a lot done . . . there was just a lot of material there; this writer, you know, writes too much instead of too little; I couldn't pass it because it was too long

Antonyms: the essays get shorter and shorter; to turn in a page and a half [length essay], that's like a sin in my class; I wouldn't pass it . . . just on length alone . . . that's a little pet peeve of mine; it would be really hard to pass a one-page paper; the first paper is too short; but aren't his essays too short, I mean all of them?; what about length as a problem . . . On certainly the last two papers?; it's a little short, but she really dealt with the problem; she just [is] always really skimpy; I counted the words . . . and it's roughly two-thirds of the minimum

Given that it is the most obvious Textual Feature of all, it's not surprising to find overall *Length/Amount (of Text)* substantially discussed in the program. Evaluators wanted to see a substantial amount of text generated, and they were pleased when texts delivered on that expectation. More interesting, perhaps, are the ways in which this important criterion qualified and also linked with other criteria.

One of the first things I noticed about participants' discussions of *Length/Amount* was how judges worked actively to qualify and contextualize that criterion so that students would neither pass nor fail solely on the basis of how many words their texts presented. All of the following comments qualifying the impact of *Length* came from the end-term (portfolio) meeting of Trio A-1:

> I couldn't pass it because it was too long.
>
> ***
>
> She writes an abundance, but a lot of what she's putting in there seemed totally irrelevant to me to what she was saying.
>
> ***
>
> It's a little short, but she really dealt with the problem.

Even though *Length* is highly important, evaluators were chary of letting it play too big a role, perhaps precisely because it is the quickest and easiest criterion by which to judge a text and can be employed using the most cursory of readings—or, in fact, without reading the text at all.

One of participants' favorite strategies for limiting the influence of *Length* in their pass/fail decisions was to link *Length* with other criteria. A prime example of this approach lies in the association between *Length* and the Contextual Criterion *Learning/Progress/Growth.* At the end of the term, when portfolios came before them, instructors noted with interest whether those portfolios demonstrated *Learning/Progress/Growth* of various kinds from the first to the last text. And *Length/Amount* was one of the most frequently invoked signs of *Progress*—or of decline.

> Also, the essays get shorter and shorter. And that more than anything was the deciding factor for me [in deciding to fail Portfolio #4]. (A Port Norm, 1293)

As my later discussion of *Learning/Progress/Growth* (chapter 4, "Contextual Criteria") explains, the narrative template of steady and continuous improvement powerfully shaped instructors' judgments of portfolios. And *Length* was among the most obvious and powerful indicators of *Progress*. Even here, however, some instructors saw the need to contextualize and reinterpret the significance of *Length*.

> The last paper should be the longest, but it's also the end of the quarter and length doesn't always mean everything. (Veronica 2)

Length could also be a mark of "engagement," one of the key synonyms for the lead criteria of Textual Quality, *Significance/Development/Heart.*

> One reason [in favor of an essay in Portfolio #4] is that there's a lot more material. The person is really engaged in this topic. She's very into it.(A Port Norm, 1334)

When a later essay offered more text than an earlier essay, one explanation was that the author became more engaged and more fluid in composing the later essay. For some evaluators, the importance of the criterion *Length* was also explicitly limited in the context of in-class essays, for which writing time was strictly limited.

> Especially for the in-class paper, I don't think [length is] quite as crucial. (A Port Norm, 1420)

***

> The [length of the] in-class essay doesn't bother me as much as the one previous to that where they had time.(A Port Norm, 1428)

In all these ways, participants limited, qualified, and contextualized the importance of *Length/Amount (of Text)* when judging essays and portfolios at City University. It was as if, knowing how powerful and yet superficial a criterion *Length* could be, they wished to prevent it from shading out other, more significant rhetorical values. As a result, they resisted judging by *Length* alone and consistently counterbalanced and alloyed it with other Textual Criteria in reaching their judgments of students' textual performances.

Content/Topic/Subject. Student writers must be warned that instructor-evaluators are likely to read their students' essays with severe irritability and grouchiness regarding a cluster of "Terrible Topics." City University's top five Terrible Topics included:

> Senior prom
> Spring break in Florida
> My boyfriend
> High school graduation
> The Big Game (baseball, football, basketball, etc.)

(Appendix A, "Assignments for English 1 Essays," illustrates how the assignments may have encouraged such well-worn subjects for students' essays.) English 1 instructors at City University were not unsympathetic to authors of essays on these topics. They recognized that, for student-authors and perhaps even for a student-audience, such topics might be profoundly meaningful and compelling.

> That's always so hard for me to figure out whether or not to pass just based on the fact that the paper's so boring, but then some of the other students think that that's interesting, 'cause they've just experienced it. (Penelope, A Mid Norm, 1040)

Nevertheless, instructors acknowledge that they see so many essays on these topics—or, perhaps more to the point, that most essays on these topics are so frighteningly alike—that they can't enjoy them or find in them most of the Textual Qualities they most admire and value.

To their credit, instructor-evaluators' responses to this predicament were reflective and inquiring, not punitive or dismissive. They debated whether content should be considered at all when evaluating students' work, yet the inescapable reality of their experience as reader-evaluators was that Terrible Topics sent a chill through them that inevitably affected their judgment.

The gravity and complexity of Terrible Topics in the evaluative dynamics of this writing program call for open discussion of the issue among instructor-evaluators in an attempt to set program policy and, at the very least, for instructors to inform students of the Top Ten Terrible Topics so they can choose topics knowing the relative risks associated with them. Widely publicizing Terrible Topics and their hazards would also presumably make instructors' lives more enjoyable because it would encourage students to range more widely in their selection and treatment of topics.

Objectionable characters, views, and situations. Closely related to Terrible Topics is another textual feature, *Objectionable Characters, Views, and Situations.* Although endless complaints about "political correctness" have for the most part lost their cultural credibility in our society over the past few years, *Objectionable Characters* will no doubt prove a politically volatile criterion, for it introduces issues of free vs. responsible speech.

Instructors sometimes complained that characters, views, or situations in students' essays were sexist, classist, racist, or violent. The most widely discussed example was the essay "Cheers" from Portfolio #3, a sample text for end-term norming. The most problematic passage from this Profile of the famous TV series from the 1980s and 1990s was the closing sentence, which was also the closing paragraph:

> When I turn on the T.V. I want to see a beautiful girl, and for the past three years I have and so has America.

The author of "Cheers" also described the waitress in the series as "an ugly brown-haired girl with five children named Clara" and ridiculed the character played by Diane Chambers for her intellectual and literary ambitions. In this context, instructor-evaluators found the essay, in Terri's mock-furious words, "sexist and anti-intellectual!" In my interview with Laura, she described the essay as "nauseating" and "the biggest piece of patriarchy I've ever seen on paper." In the next breath, however, Laura pulled herself up short:

> That's where I think you do need to be careful and blur your eyes and see where the movements are in a paper rather than what the content always is, because the content can get you into trouble. (Laura 193)

To avoid "trouble," Laura wants to dramatically curtail the influence of content in judgments of students' writing. Veronica, one of the most theoretically and politically progressive among my participants, went even further than Laura. Rather than ignoring the problematic content of the paper, Veronica saw great pedagogical potential in "Cheers."

> I know people failed ["Cheers"] because it's sexist and so on, but in my class we talked about that essay and we talked about how this writer could have . . . said that a lot of attraction and desires are mobilized by the use of glamorous women and it has this kind of effect. It seems to me that there's a way to make even those criteria persuasive. We talked about that. (Veronica 1, 955)

Veronica would neither condemn the sexism of "Cheers" nor overlook it. She would coach the author on how to take an evaluative criterion (the physical beauty of the lead actress) that came across in one draft as offensively sexist and shift it to a more sophisticated analysis that would make a similar point with similar data, but in a way that would engage, rather than offend, the intellect and sensibilities of university instructor-evaluators.

Whichever of these responses to objectionable discourse they ended up endorsing, instructors and administrators needed to talk through the tension between their appropriate and justified contempt for ignorant, elitist, violent, racist, sexist, homophobic discourse and an evaluative framework that does not punish authors because their worldviews diverge from their instructor's or their evaluators'. Then they needed to inform English 1 students of the outcome of their discussion.

Detail/Description/Examples/Dialogue. Synonyms for this Textual Feature included

> physical description; descriptive powers; details; examples; dialogue; sense of observation; vivid pictures of what we were passing through; he has this weird detail eye where he picks up on bizarre things; well observed and captured; imagery

Teachers of writing frequently impress upon their students the importance of providing *Detail/Description/Examples/Dialogue* to bring their writing to life, to make it compelling and convincing. Data from City University indicate that this criterion was quite important in that writing program and that a majority of the time the presence of this textual feature worked in the student-author's favor.

I like the details of that first essay really a lot. (A Port Norm, 1267)

***

She does the dialogue well. (Admin Pre-Port Norm, 722)

***

I was thrilled to see the descriptive powers . . . (C Mid Norm, 1021)

***

I think there's power in this writer's sense of observation. (C Mid Norm, 1293)

***

I would have liked to have had more vivid detail about the landscape (C Mid Norm, 1821)

In these cases, both when instructors found strong *Detail/Description/ Examples/Dialogue* and when they missed finding it, they valued it very positively.

About one time in four (eleven out of forty excerpts coded), however, the presence of *Detail* worked against writers. When a reader felt that the author had inserted dialogue, examples, or description "mechanically," the presence of those features counted against the text and its author. Complaining about the failure of the sample essay "Pups" to "add up" or "hold together," Veronica explained,

> I don't have a clue about what this relationship is about. You know, not from the description, not from what they talk about, not from the argument, and not from the ending. (A Mid Norm, 585)

Veronica repeatedly lamented what she saw as "mechanical" insertion of *Detail/Description/Examples/Dialogue* into texts. Later in the term, Kevin expressed similar reservations about the essay "When Thinking" from sample Portfolio #2.

> When she describes Lela, I get no picture of Lela at all. It's like, "Her appearance is deceiving: five nine, curly brown hair, baby blue eyes, big smile, great skin," you know, she doesn't sort of have an overall characterization of Lela to sort of form an impression in my mind. (Admin Pre-Port Norm, 843)

As in the cases of *Revision* and *Significance* (among other criteria), studying *Detail* reveals unexpected nuances and dynamics that cry out for further discussion and decision making among instructors and for providing fuller information for students.

Dynamic Criteria Mapping of evaluative discourse at City University revealed that the dominant group of criteria for judgment in this writing program were *Textual.* That is, judges of students' writing most often made their pass/fail decisions based on their experiences and perceptions of the texts being judged. This chapter has explored four main findings regarding this writing program's textual criteria for evaluation:

1.   Textual criteria could be either *qualities* or *features*
2.   Textual criteria were numerous, multifaceted, and responsive to rhetorical context
3.   Dynamics, nuances, tensions, and conflicts were at work *within* individual textual criteria
4.   The interplay *among* textual criteria was also dynamic, nuanced, and sometimes controversial

While these findings are rewarding and useful, they cover relatively familiar ground in writing assessment. We expect the judgment of writing to be based in the qualities and features of the texts being judged. The following chapter explores less familiar territory: judgments of student writing being shaped by criteria that have nothing to do with the specific texts being assessed. At the same time they pondered Textual Criteria while trying to reach decisions, evaluators at City University also grappled with Contextual Criteria. In other words, nearly as often as the difference between "pass" and "fail" depended on a text's *Mechanics, Revision,* or *Unity* (for example), it hinged on such considerations as *Goals for English 1,* a *Construction of the Writer,* or evaluators' views of appropriate *Standards and Expectations* for their students. Judgments of texts were therefore also judgments of contexts.

4

CONTEXTUAL CRITERIA
What They Really Valued, Part 2

When explaining their pass/fail judgments of students' texts, instructors at City University most often pointed to the "qualities" or "features" of those texts (see chapter 3, "Textual Criteria"). However, another substantial portion of participants' discussions focused on criteria for evaluation [5] not directly concerned with the text currently under judgment. These Contextual Criteria demonstrated how pedagogical, ethical, collegial, and other aspects of the environment surrounding students' texts guided and shaped evaluators' decisions.

Rarely do scoring guides venture into the realm of evaluative context when investigating or reporting on how rhetorical judgments are made. Traditional rubrics much more commonly delineate Textual Criteria for evaluation than they do Contextual Criteria. Our profession is accustomed to thinking of evaluation in textual terms, but not contextual ones. In light of this subdisciplinary habit, Jane Mathison Fife and Peggy O'Neill call for a shift "from a textual focus to a contextual one" in the practice and research of responding to students' writing.

> [A] problem with recent response studies is the tendency to view comments from the researcher's perspective alone, analyzing the comments as a *text* apart from the classroom *context* that gave rise to them. (300, emphasis original)

By analyzing criteria drawn from the evaluative context for participants' pass/fail decisions, this chapter takes up Fife and O'Neill's challenge in the specific realm of evaluation.

As we will see, at City University, Contextual Criteria were often viewed as illegitimate, inappropriate, or contraband and, therefore, kept secret or hidden. If these hidden criteria are, in fact, in play, however, we need to render them visible so they can be discussed, negotiated, and then made available publicly, especially to our students. Dynamic Criteria Mapping can document and bring to light evaluative systems of which composition faculty might otherwise remain unaware (or about which they prefer to remain silent), including the previously unexplored realm of Contextual Criteria.

Table 4, "City University's Contextual Criteria," presents the twenty-two Contextual Criteria invoked by administrators and instructor-evaluators to explain, defend, and advocate for their decisions to pass or fail students' texts.

As in table 2, "Quantitative Analysis of All Criteria for Judgment" (from which table 4 is excerpted), Contextual Criteria are listed here in quantitative order, from the most- to the least-discussed criteria as measured by the total number of transcript lines coded for each criterion.

STANDARDS AND EXPECTATIONS

The most frequent contextual guide for judgments was the issue of how "high" evaluators' expectations of students' rhetorical performances should be. Only to the Textual Criterion *Mechanics* did participants devote more time than to the Contextual Criterion *Standards*. It is also worth noting that *Mechanics* is actually comprised of eight subcriteria; *Standards/Expectations* may therefore legitimately be counted the single most frequently discussed criterion in City University's portfolio program.

To decide whether a text should pass or fail, instructors needed to know not only how "good" was the rhetorical performance presented in the text, but also how good they should *expect* that performance to be. As I have described in a previous study (Broad 2000), participants' effort to establish a clear and stable "borderline" between pass and fail was extremely difficult and problematic. My current analysis of *Standards/Expectations* reveals three specific dynamics by which *Standards* systematically shifted: *What English 1 is About*, *Indeterminate Borders* between passing and failing, and *Shifting Borders*. These considerations help to explain why *Standards* refused to be as solid, stable, and portable an entity as participants wished.

"A Really Serious Question": What English 1 is About

The most urgent and compelling question underlying *Standards/Expectations* also unfortunately turned out to be unanswerable. Participants tried, but failed, to determine what English 1 is about.

During the end-term norming session for Team A, an instructor named Edwina interrupted the discussion of various Textual Criteria informing participants' pass/fail judgments of Portfolio #2 with an

Table 4

City University's Contextual Criteria

Standards/Expectations
Constructing Writers
Fulfilling the Assignment
Learning/Progress/Growth
Plagiarism/Originality
Nature of Pass/Fail Judgment
Essay vs. Portfolio
Ready for English 2
Benefit to Student
Non-text Factors
*
Goals for English 1
Difficulty of the Writing Task
Writing Center
Fairness/Hypocrisy
Writer Shows Promise
Cultural Differences
Using the Spell Check
Constructing Teachers
Compassion for Writer
Time
Turned in Late
Attendance

*   Empty rows in this table divide the list of criteria into visually and mathematically meaningful groups of ten.

inquiry that cut to the heart of the issue of *Standards/Expectations* and forcefully introduced Contextual Criteria into the discussion:

> I thought this [portfolio] was very borderline. At first I passed it, and then I said . . . Is this what we consider COMPETENCY? And I guess it depends on how you look at why we're using the portfolio system. If we're using it to just sort of pass people along unless they're really in desperate shape, then it passes. . . . But if we're using it to say . . . let's give kids more work where they need it. Let's not get 'em into English 2 where now they're really in desperate shape and they're floundering because the ideas are so difficult to grapple with and they still haven't kind of gotten the basic. I felt like this writer was like on the edge. (A Port Norm 706)

Focusing on the great pedagogical potential of "the portfolio system," Edwina favored using English 1 to thoroughly prepare City University's students for English 2 and the rest of the university experience. She was uncomfortable following administrators' directives to set her expectations low enough to pass Portfolio #2 because she believed its author would flounder if allowed to proceed through the FYE sequence. To know how to set her standards (that is, whether to pass Portfolio #2), she needed to know which way (minimal preparation or substantial preparation) English 1 should function in the FYE Program and the University.

Terri, leader of Team A's norming sessions, immediately acknowledged the fundamental importance of Edwina's question. "You raise a really serious question that's at the basis of everything we do." At the same time, however, Terri admitted that "I can't address it, you know? I think maybe Emily [director of the FYE Program] could address it?" And with that Team A moved on to discuss other matters.

In later interviews, Terri observed that "Edwina brought up the, you know, mother of all questions." But Terri "didn't feel that [she] could give her an answer to that question." Terri believed Edwina's statement was "absolutely the thing to talk about, but that this [norming session] was not the time to talk about it," even though, Terri admitted, "how you resolve that question for yourself determines . . . the evaluations that you make." This formulation of Terri's provides a superb definition of Contextual Criteria for evaluation and indicates how powerful they were in shaping high-stakes decisions.

It is not easy to see how Edwina's Big Question could be definitively answered, but it is quite clear how successfully identifying and agreeing upon *Standards/Expectations* requires such an answer. In the process of Dynamic Criteria Mapping, a writing program would take up the question in the context of course and university goals and try to describe to all concerned (students, instructors, and faculty across the curriculum) whether "basic competency" should be viewed as minimal or substantial. Unfortunately for City University's students and instructor-evaluators, they had to proceed without such guidance in the fall quarter during which I gathered data.

Indeterminate Borders

A large portion of the discourse of *Standards/Expectations* centered on how instructor- evaluators could "draw the line" or establish the "bottom line" that would aid them in distinguishing passing from failing texts. To this end, participants gathered, voted pass/fail on each sample text, and then discussed the criteria that guided their judgments. At the conclusion of the discussion of each text, the team leader (Terri, Kevin, or Emily) indicated whether "the program" felt that particular sample text should pass or fail. Two specific sample texts were meant to mark the border between pass and fail: at midterm, the essay "Gramma Sally" was declared just below passing quality; at the end of the term, Portfolio #2 was identified as just above that line.

An interesting twist on the project of delineating evaluative borders arose during end-term norming for Team A when instructors Sandra and Veronica asked team leader Terri whether the Team could discuss "what an A portfolio is." Even though norming sessions focused exclusively on pass/fail decisions and left judgments about grades (A, B, or C) to individual instructors, Veronica and Sandra felt it would help them in their trio meetings if norming sessions addressed "some standards for the A and B portfolios also" and "Where an A [portfolio] becomes a B+."

Terri responded somewhat skeptically:

> Do you think that we can actually determine such a thing? . . . I don't think that we could really as a program say, "This is an A, and this is a B." (A Port Norm 1554)

What struck me about Terri's clear sense that the A/B dividing line is indeterminate was that it corresponds perfectly with the tremendous struggle around *Standards/Expectations* to delineate the dividing line between pass/fail. Apparently, both dividing lines are equally indeterminate. Yet even as they threw up their hands in the face of the challenge of distinguishing A from B portfolios, Terri and the other team leaders enthusiastically promoted the project of establishing clear and consistent *Standards* for separating passing from failing texts, saying about various sample texts, in essence, "Let us be clear: This is a pass, and this is a fail."

Part of the problem with "drawing the line" between pass and fail was suggested in some of Terri's (and others') language: "This level of facility is what we're going to be calling passing." She approached the confusion about *Standards* as if the problem was that colleagues couldn't agree on where the dividing line between pass and fail should be set. But my analyses of City University's discussions suggest that the real problem is that different people perceive or judge different "levels of facility" for the same text because they perceive and/or value texts as meeting different textual and contextual criteria (also recall that Diederich, French, and Carlton found exactly the same thing). Rather than acknowledging the phenomenological nature of evaluation, the "standard-setting" approach treated what was really a judgment (the quality of the performance) instead as a concrete, "objective" artifact. This explains why it proved such a frustrating project for both administrators and instructors.

City University could conceivably have committed itself more fully to the rhetorical, postpositivist paradigm on which its portfolio program already drew heavily. Had it done so, it might have been able to loosen its grip on the "standard-setting" goal of securing independent and prior evaluative agreement among evaluators. Instead, the program could have invested in open discussion of the various criteria instructors valued in norming sessions and in deliberative debate within trios. Such discussions and debates, with which City University's program was rich, led to highly valid and informative judgments without the need for elaborate or rigid systems for fixing *Standards* that are not, in the nature of rhetorical experience, fixed objects.

"But the World Intrudes": Shifting Borders

At other times, when participants in City University's FYE Program were not focused on fixing standards, they saw important reasons that *Standards/Expectations* should not, in fact, be fixed but should instead move in response to changing pedagogical contexts. One example of appropriately shifting standards was the idea that judges should be "tougher" or "stricter" at the midterm and then ease their expectations down somewhat when they made their final judgments on students' portfolios at the end of the term.

During Team C's midterm norming session, Kevin recommended this strategy to the TAs who made up his Seminar in the Teaching of Writing and who also comprised Team C. He explained why it made sense to set standards higher at the midterm.

> [T]his is the midterm evaluation, okay? And just because a paper doesn't pass the midterm evaluation, that doesn't have that much to do with whether or not the student is gonna pass at the end of the quarter, okay? So in a way we can be a little more strict now than we are later, because [INAUDIBLE] send a message to students. (C Mid Norm 78)

To support the message he wants instructors to send to their students (work harder on your remaining papers, and consider revising this one), Kevin encourages his TAs to start high with their expectations and bring them down, as necessary and appropriate, at the end of the course.

So midterm *Standards* were set higher than those at the end of the term. In another theorized shift in *Expectations,* norming sessions were more rigorous than the trio sessions whose decisions norming was intended to shape. To understand this more complex dynamic, it will help if we recall several ways in which norming sessions and trio sessions differed.

	Norming Sessions	*Trio Meetings*
Nature of texts being evaluated	Sample texts authored by students from past years' sections of English 1	"Live" texts authored by students currently enrolled in trio-mates' sections
Size of group	Large group: 15–20 instructors	Three (or occasionally two) instructors
Discussion leader	FYE Program administrator: Terri, Kevin, or Emily	No administrators present

One explanation for higher expectations in norming came from Kevin, who attributed it to a difference between norming's "abstract" evaluations and the "concrete" character of trio meetings:

> I think in the abstract, it's always easier to have stricter standards. . . . In a concrete, everyday situation with students in your own class, or someone else's students where, this student would have to repeat the course, and it's expensive, and it's discouraging, and—but the world intrudes. (Kevin 3, 280)

When Kevin observes how "the world intrudes" into trio-members' decisions, he is noting that in trios the real-life consequences of their "live" decisions help to shape rhetorical judgments. Trio C-6 experienced exactly this sort of intrusion when Laura and Ted, during their end-term trio meeting, found themselves "trying not to think about" the extra time and money demanded of a student who would fail English 1.

Decisions made in norming sessions, by contrast, had no real-life consequences for the student-authors of the sample texts being judged. Instead, the most important consequences of norming discussions are those affecting instructors and administrators. TA Martin explained how.

Martin began by making the same general observation as Kevin: that norming sessions were "stricter" or "harsher".

> [T]he norming sessions we had . . . kind of threw me. I thought people were a little harsher than I expected. (Martin 1, 8)

And initially Martin offered an explanation similar to Kevin's of why sample texts (in norming) were judged more harshly than live texts (in trios):

> [I]f we fail this person it doesn't matter, we're not really affecting them. It seemed they were a little bit harsher [in norming sessions]. (Martin 1, 23)

Martin agreed with Kevin that the absence of personal consequences for norming decisions led judges to be more demanding in that setting.

However, Martin also had a distinct additional explanation for those higher expectations, one having to do less with norming's lack of ethical constraints and more with competition among evaluators for professional status. He commented,

> it almost seemed to me that in [norming sessions] people are almost trying to out-class other people, like "Hey, I got this error and this error." (Martin 1, 81)

In other words, Martin hypothesized that norming sessions featured "harsher" judgments partly because his peers on Team C were competing to identify and punish more errors in the sample texts as a means of gaining status among the group of new TAs who comprised Team C, as well as in the eyes of Kevin, the associate director of the FYE Program, who led Team C and who was simultaneously their professor for the Seminar. Martin's team- and trio-mate Laura concurred with Martin's sense of norming as a distinctively demanding evaluative context due to the political dynamics of norming Teams.

> [Y]ou definitely [would] much rather raise your hand to fail a student than you would pass a student [in norming]. . . . the most favorable value to have is rigor, not one of ease and leniency. (Laura 873)

In contrast to norming's gladiatorial qualities, trio meetings featured more "lenient" and "generous" standards because real students' lives were affected by the outcomes. Rhonda contrasted norming, which she described as "tougher or divorced from personal contact," with trios, in which the instructor might be tempted to comment, "Oh, [this student] is such a nice person, you know." Martin described trios' distinctive evaluative processes this way:

> [W]e were more specific. I think we would . . . invest more caring than we would on something like [norming]. . . . you almost gave more benefit of the doubt to people . . . got more insight into [a student's] personality, just from the instructor. (Martin 1, 28)

Instructors may have had more at stake in attempting to set *Standards/Expectations* than in their work on any other criterion. Not only was fairness to students and professional status at stake; if they could finally "draw the line" and "set the border" between passing and failing

portfolios, they could also have saved themselves hours of agonizing over
and debating difficult evaluative decisions. As this analysis shows, however, shifting evaluative contexts brought shifting *Standards,* due to three
distinct dynamics, and it is not clear how such shifting can—or whether it
should—be finally eliminated. It may be, as Laura suggests, that the effort
to standardize evaluations must stop short of guaranteeing agreement.
Laura found that reflecting on the dynamics of *Standards/Expectations:*

> makes you question whether there's a universal writing standard or whether
> you standardize within the context of the classroom, or within a department.
> (Laura, C-6 Mid Trio 1997)

In the end, the level of performance we expect from students in a given
context may be inevitably linked to issues of pedagogy, ethics, and professional status like those in which City University's writing instructors found
themselves entangled. If so, we will have to get used to shifting evaluative
borders, for the professional contexts on the basis of which those borders
are surveyed and mapped will always be manifold and varied.

FULFILLING THE ASSIGNMENT: THE GATEWAY CRITERION

Alone among Contextual Criteria one finds *Fulfilling the Assignment*
often mentioned on traditional rubrics (notice the criterion "addresses
the question fully" in White's rubric presented near the outset of chapter
1). Though I have never seen this criterion acknowledged as Contextual
and therefore different in character and function from Textual Criteria,
nevertheless it is named on many scoring guides and rubrics.

This criterion was also unique it its gatekeeping role in assessment discussions in the FYE Program. If a text was judged not to fulfill the assignment for which it was submitted, then no other judgment of the text's
other virtues mattered: the text would fail regardless. However, instructor-
evaluators did not agree on when or even whether the distinctive and
potent gatekeeping function of *Fulfilling the Assignment* should be invoked.

At City University, a writer got into trouble if her essay seemed to fulfill another assignment better than the one she claimed or appeared to
be trying to fulfill. She also encountered trouble if the evaluator
couldn't tell which assignment the text aimed to fulfill ("significant
event" vs. "portrait" was the most common confusion among assignments). During Team C's midterm norming session, Kent clearly stated,

> I'm assuming that "Pops" and "Belle" and "Gramma Sally," those were all the
> portrait? Or maybe that "Pops" was a significant event? Or, I wasn't . . . If it
> was one I'd pass it, if it was the other I wouldn't, so . . . (C Mid Norm 254)

For Kent, *Fulfilling the Assignment* was a crucial criterion that could, alone, determine whether the student-author passed or failed. Yet Veronica, a graduate teaching assistant on Team A, admitted that she herself had difficulty distinguishing between the important person and the "profile" assignments.

> Um, I think I have confused my students because it was hard for them to distinguish sometimes between a significant person and a profile and I even had the same [problem]. (A-1 Port Trio, 191)

If some instructors were not clear about the differences among the assignments, we might legitimately wonder whether their students should be passed or failed on the basis of their ability to distinguish clearly among the assignments.

The appropriateness of *Fulfilling the Assignment* as a gatekeeping criterion was questioned more emphatically by Laura, a graduate TA on Team C. In the midterm meeting of her trio (C-6), Laura introduced her strong and clear position on the topic of *Fulfilling the Assignment* as a special and powerful criterion for judging students' writing.

> I don't think how a student treats the topic should be even a CLOSE factor as to where we place the student? . . . As long as the student presents a creation that fulfills its own goal. (Laura, C-6 Mid Trio 455)

During Team C end-term (portfolio) norming, Laura took this concern to the larger group of her colleagues:

> It's come up time and again, like, "did they meet the assignment?". . . And I just think that we have to be careful about the criteria we use when we're talking about papers and students constructing meaning from a prompt. . . . I think this paper ["Gram" from sample Portfolio #1] comes close enough to what it is we want students to do, and for some reason I felt compelled to say that out loud because, I'm not sure that we are going to be able to direct how students should construct meaning. I just feel real strongly about that. (Laura, C Port Norm 758)

Finally, in her end-term trio meeting, she made this more startling confession:

> I like to let them [students] learn what it's like to create a form to support their papers in some ways so their papers are—and actually I changed all my assignments and modified them in different ways [LAUGHS]. (Laura, C-6 Port Trio 619)

Laura's constructivist pedagogy required significant relaxation of this major criterion for evaluation, since presumably students would construct and fulfill "standard" assignments (see appendix A) in diverse ways. When, like Laura, an instructor exercised her authority to reinterpret and tailor the assignments and empowered her students to "create the form to support their papers," judging students first and foremost by whether they fulfilled the assignment seemed even more problematic.

Needless to say, not all of Laura's colleagues shared her views. Subsequent to her last speech, quoted above, during the end-term meeting of Trio C-6, Laura's trio-mate Ted announced that he saw a particular essay as off topic and he therefore failed it. Apparently Ted did not embrace Laura's theory and practice of constructivist evaluation.   .

Due to the sharp philosophical, pedagogical, and evaluative differences at play around the gateway criterion *Fulfilling the Assignment,* I believe it urgently deserved the attention of the City University FYE Program. These teachers of writing needed to decide how they would evaluate texts that might fulfill assignments in ways substantially different from how they themselves interpreted and taught those assignments. With the help of Dynamic Criteria Mapping, instructors and administrators can learn about problematic criteria like this one, discuss them, and negotiate a position for the program that addresses these dramatic conflicts.

CONSTRUCTING WRITERS

In an attempt to alleviate the maddening ambiguity of evaluating texts, City University's instructors often fashioned contexts within which to read and judge those texts. One method of creating contexts to help point the way toward either a "pass" or "fail" decision was to construct a portrait or narrative of the student-author. Instances of *Constructing Writers* fell into two main groups: *Teachers' Special Knowledge* (an instructor sharing with trio-mates direct and exclusive knowledge about a student-author taught by the instructor) and outside instructors' *Imagined Details* about student-authors and their writing processes. Predictably, *Teachers' Special Knowledge (TSK)* predominated in trio meetings, in which each student-author's instructor was present. *Imagined Details,* on the other hand, were prevalent in norming sessions, where little or no direct knowledge of the student-author was available.

A key observation at the outset of this section is that *Constructing Writers* is a widespread and perhaps inescapable feature of reading. We always construct an ethos behind a text as a means of interpreting and evaluating that text. What is new is our awareness that we need to document such evaluative dynamics so we can hold them up to critical scrutiny and make programmatic decisions about how to handle them. Dynamic Criteria Mapping provides a method for just this sort of reflective inquiry into assessment and for action based on that inquiry.

It may also prove helpful if I emphasize the difference between the Contextual Criterion *Constructing Writers,* discussed below, and the *Ethos* constellation among Textual Criteria, discussed above in chapter 3. *Ethos* as a Textual Criterion consists of inferences drawn by readers on the basis of clues observable in the text. By contrast, *Constructing Writers* is a Contextual Criterion precisely because the clues from which readers construct these portraits or narratives of authors come from outside of the student-authored text. Those clues are instead drawn either from instructors' direct knowledge of students based on teaching them in class or from instructors' imaginations.

"That's One of the Advantages of Having the Teacher Here": Teachers' Special Knowledge

In a previous study (Broad 1997), I explored and theorized the phenomenon of Teachers' Special Knowledge, which I defined as *direct and exclusive knowledge of the student-author shared by an instructor with her or his trio-mates.* In that investigation, I looked at Teachers' Special Knowledge as one of three forms of *evaluative authority* in City University's portfolio program. *TSK* figures into the current study in a different way: as one of two methods by which evaluators provided *context for their judgments* of student-authors' performances.

Ted, a TA instructor on Team C, provided one view of the value and importance of *TSK:*

> That's one of the advantages of having the teacher here. The teacher will always will have seen a lot more of that student's work. (Ted, C-6 Port Trio 2344)

Ted felt that the teacher's wider knowledge of the student's work gave the teacher the ability to make a better judgment than outside instructors' "cold readings" alone could provide.

TSK touched on a wide variety of kinds of information about the student-authors whose texts were under discussion and judgment, including their age, appearance, gender, ethnicity, effort, writing process, attitude, personal habits, academic major, cocurricular activities, and learning disabilities. Sometimes the sharing of *TSK* appeared to make a difference in the evaluative outcome for the student concerned, but other times it appeared to serve other purposes, including building professional and personal camaraderie among trio-mates.

We might expect *TSK* to have been a tool or strategy by which instructors would try directly to influence or control the evaluative outcome of trio deliberations. While that was sometimes the case (see below), *TSK* often appeared to function very differently. Instructors more frequently offered or requested information that complicated the pedagogical and evaluative scene rather than clarifying it. In these cases, instructors seemed more interested in reaching the best decision or getting their trio-mates' professional counsel and camaraderie than in advocating one judgment or another.

In the midterm meeting of Trio A-1, Veronica explained why she was relieved that her trio-mates passed an essay by one of her (Veronica's) students. It is important to note that Veronica shared this *TSK after* her trio had reached its "pass" decision on the essay in question.

> I think he would benefit more from getting the pass, because he's kind of anti-authoritarian. It's taken him a lot to open out and really work in the class. . . . I know that if he fails he's going to quit trying. (A-1 Mid Trio 840)

Veronica believed that her trio's decision would help her student keep trying in English 1, and she retrospectively shared this contextual insight. Shortly after this exchange, Veronica's trio-mate Sandra offered similar, after-the-fact context for her trio's decision to "just barely" pass an essay written by one of her (Sandra's) students.

> [H]e did start out okay, but it's like maybe he spent a couple of evenings working on the first half of his paper, and then, the night before it was due, he whipped out that third page. (A-1 Mid Trio 1045)

Sandra was not campaigning to fail this student, but rather explaining why it would be useful to her to pass along to the student Veronica's message that she would "pass it, but just barely." Sandra hoped that the "just barely" warning would spur the student to put in more effort and do more revision.

Additional *TSK* shared in this portfolio program seemed unrelated to the pass/fail decision and appeared rooted in plain curiosity by readers about student-authors.

Veronica: Is she an older woman?

Rhonda: Just a little bit, I think. It's hard for me to tell. . . . She's in her thirties, I guess. (A-1 Port Trio 969)

And the complex little exchange below among the members of Trio A-1 explicated some of the sources, effects, and limitations of *TSK,* including the student-authors' race or ethnicity and whether and why a reader would need to know that information.

Sandra: Is Lyle black?

Veronica: Yeah.

Rhonda: I thought that was interesting, that one [essay] on the racism thing. Because you don't know. It's like, well why should you know? It's racism either way.

Sandra: Yeah, I know, but I was curious. [LAUGHS] (A-1 Port Trio 1924)

Characteristically, Rhonda argued in this excerpt for the value of instructors' *not* sharing *TSK,* while Sandra frankly admitted that her inquiry had no more profound basis than curiosity.

In the other core-group trio (Trio C-6), *TSK* followed dynamics similar to those observed in Trio A-1. Laura shared *TSK* to explain her ambivalence about a paper and to try to figure out the decision that would send the "right message" to its author, one of her students:

[Y]ou wouldn't believe the jump from draft one and draft two, but . . . Part of me—I guess I felt like I'd be giving her the wrong message [if I passed her]. (C-6 Mid Trio 2007)

Discussing the portfolio of one of his own students, Ted offered *TSK* that complicated an evaluation on which he and Martin had already agreed:

[She's o]ne of my funnier students. She's a real pain, though. . . . She just has an attitude. A real attitude. (C-6 Port Trio 504)

Martin then took a turn at *TSK,* sharing one of his student's idiosyncrasies without any apparent desired impact on the pass/fail judgment.

He's almost paranoid about grammar. That he's gonna make a mistake, and he'll come and ask me about stuff. I think he just, people must have told him before that you need to do this this way. (C-6 Port Trio 547)

Later, when Martin strongly felt one of Ted's students' portfolios should fail and Laura "timidly passed" the same portfolio, Ted employed *TSK* to explain how he would resolve the dispute. This student, Ted said,

> seemed to me not to show any real understanding of how language works. I mean she just seemed to wing it, and I felt like she was, she was getting toward unteachable? You know, she was kind of hermetic. You know, "This is the way I do it and I can't even imagine any other way to do it"? I was afraid I was going to run into that with her. But she did pull it out. She did manage to learn quite a bit and her writing improved. So I thought, yeah, this is passing writing. But I was very nervous about it because of her earlier writing. (C 6 Port Trio 2366)

Here, Ted's deep ambivalence seems to legitimize his trio-mates' disagreement and also explain why Ted is comfortable passing it with reservations. Whereas most criteria for evaluation at City University were discussed in an apparent effort to advocate for one evaluative decision or another, the examples of *TSK* presented above appeared to serve a more reflective, inquiring, community-building function.

At other times, *TSK* appeared to be a tactic by which an instructor would attempt to persuade his or her trio toward one decision or another. The following statements all appear intended (or, in any case, likely) to improve the student's chance of passing.

> She's just a sweetheart (Veronica, A-1 Mid Trio 394)

> I think this is a difficult issue because he's a really bright kid but he has dialect interference, or whatever you would call that. (Veronica, A-1 Mid Trio 783)

> *Sandra:* Yeah, she's a real good writer. Sweet kid, too.
> *Veronica:* Oh, what a winning combination. [LAUGHS]
> *Sandra:* [LAUGHS] Well, I wish all my students were like her.
>   (A-1 Port Trio 130)

> She's the most imaginative writer I've got. (Ted, C-6 Mid Trio 1454)

> These two students worked really hard on those, too. (Laura, C-6 Mid Trio 1793)

> I think he works for hours on these things. (Ted, C-6 Port Trio 1112)

Perhaps more dramatic were those instances in which instructors' *TSK* seemed likely to lead to a "fail" judgment from their trio-mates. For example, when judging an essay by one of Veronica's students, Sandra said she would pass the essay but admitted she was having trouble making up her mind. So Veronica helped her.

> I would really love to teach him a lesson. . . . He drives me nuts. He's kind of this big jock guy. . . . I told him that he would have to convince me that this guy [the subject of the student's "important person" essay] was really special if he says things like, "Women are like buses," and stuff like that. . . . And, thing is that both his papers had the same errors. To me, you know, that's very significant. He doesn't really try in there. . . . I was hoping somebody would flunk him. (A-1 Mid Trio 1122)

After hearing Veronica's comments on her frustrations with and resentments toward the student, Sandra revisited the essay and decided it should fail after all.

> Now that I'm looking at all the comments I've made about this paper, I'm really not sure I would pass it because, in a sense, if he's got the comma splice and the spelling errors and the fragments, he really doesn't even have the basic skills down pat. (Sandra, A-1 Mid Trio 1152)

Again at the end of the term, Veronica poured forth her complaints about a different student.

> You know, they had four absences, I mean, I had him write an extra paper, but I didn't allow him to put it in there. It's all about reverse racism. . . . This is a kid that acts up in class all the time. (Veronica, A-1 Port Trio 818)

When Sandra ironically commented that "I can tell you were fond of this student," Veronica added,

> Well, aside from the fact that he would chew tobacco and spit it out in the can the whole quarter, you know. Just a very juvenile kid. (A-1 Port Trio 818)

Later in the same trio meeting, even Rhonda, who generally resisted and challenged *TSK* (see below), shared it with her trio-mates. Sandra, again struggling to reach her decision, had said she would pass one of Rhonda's students, Rhonda replied:

> Oh, rats. [LAUGHS] I don't think he learned a thing the whole quarter. (A-1 Port Trio 2306)

In response to Rhonda's comment, Sandra reviewed the many weaknesses of this student's portfolio but concluded that "it's still passing.

Barely, but it's passing." Rhonda's *TSK* apparently failed to influence Sandra's judgment.

Trio C-6 also participated in negative *TSK.*

> This girl came in to [see] me first day of class and asked if she could do creative writing. And I said, "No." So the problem here is that she's still trying to do creative writing. (Ted, C-6 Mid Trio 1533)

> Well, the reason they're both in borderline is because I have seen them produce terrible writing. (Ted, C-6 Mid Trio 2165)

In these instances, instructors introduced positive or negative *TSK* into trio discussions in an apparent attempt to influence the evaluative outcome for their students.

In reflecting on *TSK* dynamics, we should keep in mind two important problems with its use. First, the program's administrators expressly directed instructor-evaluators to reach their decisions based on "the text alone," and explicitly *without* reference to *TSK.* Therefore, as a criterion for judgment of students' work, *TSK* was contraband. Second, outside evaluators (those trio-mates who lacked direct knowledge of the student-author) had no means by which to assess the accuracy, fairness, or appropriateness of any *TSK* that might be interject into a trio discussion. *TSK* was therefore also suspect and sometimes openly resisted (see below). Despite both these limitations, *TSK* was a powerful and pervasive part of the evaluative process in this portfolio program and was one of two important means by which judges framed their pass/fail decisions by *Constructing Writers.*

The crucial issue for Dynamic Criteria Mapping is to reveal the presence and character of *TSK.* Once this influential Contextual Criterion is documented and understood, writing instructors and administrators can discuss whether and how to use it appropriately in assessing students' performances. And if a writing program does authorize *TSK* as a criterion for evaluation, its students must be informed and helped to understand how *TSK* may determine the evaluation of their written work.

Imagined Details

Though *TSK* is in some ways more dramatic because of its illicit status in the writing program, I find the other method of *Constructing Writers* even more provocative. *Imagined Details* intrigues me because it involves evaluators' fictional portrayals of student-authors' lives. As I mentioned above, while *TSK* typified the discourse of trio meetings, in which teachers could share direct knowledge about their students, *Imagined Details* was the dominant mode of *Constructing Writers* in norming sessions, where (with one or two exceptions) the authors of sample texts were complete strangers to every reader present.

Even in norming, where no one could credibly provide juicy tidbits about the author's age, writing processes, ethnicity, effort, character, personal habits, appearance, or attitudes, evaluators often supplied those details for themselves. They frequently inferred, imagined, or simply assumed "facts" about a student-author and her composition processes. Often these fictionalized details helped point evaluators toward one decision or another, thus speeding and easing their tasks.

Norming discussions featured relatively little of the exploratory, inquiring, complicating discourse of *Constructing Writers* that played a substantial role in trio meetings. Since norming sessions were a more strictly evaluative and less pedagogical evaluative context, efforts to construct writers in norming focused more exclusively on persuading the group either to pass or to fail the sample text under discussion. In Aristotelian terms, the rhetoric of norming sessions was more thoroughly *deliberative* than that of trios.

In Team A midterm norming, Sandra voted with a large majority of participants to pass the sample text "Pops." In defending her passing vote against Veronica's critique that the essay was formulaic and trite, Sandra argued that the author's young age and lack of experience made it impossible for her (the author) to write a more innovative or intellectually substantive essay.

> I would chalk that up to them being 17 years old, you know? . . . and not really having a whole lot to write about. (A Mid Norm 745)

While clues in "Pops" suggest that the writer is likely a traditional student and therefore quite young, the essay does not say so explicitly. And the text gives no indication as to her breadth of worldly experience. Sandra is supplying an imagined biographical detail about the author—specifically, her youth and inexperience—in support of her vote to pass "Pops."

In a close parallel to arguments made in Team A, Renee of Team C deflects criticisms of "Pops" by defending the author's lack of maturity against critique and judgment.

> [O]ne of the things I thought about when I read this was that you can't really make somebody more mature than they are? You know, and so within the context of who this person is as she reveals herself in this, she kind of does

the best job that she can with it? . . . I don't think you can really ask her to change her maturity overnight. I think she does a good job with what she's got. (C Mid Norm 1829)

Without any direct knowledge of the student-author or her level of maturity, Renee imagined the student's emotional and psychological profile and defended "Pops" on that basis.

In another norming session, Florence made a parallel argument in defense of "Gramma Sally." Though Florence voted with "half a hand" to fail this sample essay, she also volunteered to speak on its behalf. In so doing, she constructed a psychological predicament for the author that excused the psychological contradictions, which, along with the essay's stylistic and mechanical problems, troubled a slight majority of instructors in the program enough to fail the essay.

> I don't believe that [the contradiction is] necessarily the fault of her as a writer; it may be the fault of her experience. . . . I think that she's got an experience here that she really hasn't worked through. . . . I think she's reporting this experience, and it's a TERRIBLE experience. . . . She's eighteen years old, and she doesn't know what else to do with it. . . . yes, I think she is sincere. (A Mid Norm 819)

For Florence, the "sincere" writer has endured a psychologically traumatic experience so recently that she (the author) ought not to be criticized for the raw and conflicting emotions recounted in the essay. Here again we see an evaluator fashioning a biographical circumstance for the student-author, a circumstance that was reasonably inferred from the text (assuming that the text is a reliable representation of events) but that also remained speculative and unconfirmed.

During Team C's midterm norming session, Kevin added a dimension to Florence's analysis of the author of "Gramma Sally." Though Kevin believed the essay should fail, he also wanted to acknowledge its strengths.

> It's rich with detail, it's full of good examples, it's lively, it's interesting. The writer is clearly deeply engaged in the topic. It's not a perfunctory effort at all, you know? And that's clear. It jumps off the page how she's wrestling to come to grips with her feelings about this complex old woman. (C Mid Norm 908)

Up to this point, Kevin had limited his observations to aspects of his direct experience with the text, that is, Textual Criteria (both Qualities and Features). Then he added an imagined or speculative detail by suggesting that the author "may resemble [the character Gramma Sally] in some respects. I mean the writer herself seems kind of tough-minded and interesting" (C Mid Norm 915).

Florence and Kevin offer the emotional closeness of the "Gramma Sally" author to the traumatic events related in the essay as evidence of the author's gutsiness and nerve. In voting with near unanimity to fail "Anguish," however, instructors counted that author's closeness to traumatic events against him/her.

> This writer's too close to the event. That's why she keeps popping back in the present tense, to me. (Mike, C Mid Norm 1313)

> [H]e's too close to the situation, he's . . . he or she is clouded by emotion. (Dorothy 1467)

The student-authors of both "Gramma Sally" and "Anguish" were described as excessively close to their material. In one case that closeness counted in the author's favor, and in the other case it counted against the author. What is most relevant at the moment is that the author's emotional or psychological distance from her content was a prime example of *Constructing Writers* through *Imagined Detail.*

When *Imagined Details* and *TSK* Clash

Having documented and explored *TSK* and *Imagined Details* as separate Contextual Criteria for judgment, we can now look at some of the dynamics surrounding and connecting these two distinct methods by which participants constructed writers. One of the most interesting of those dynamics appears when *TSK* and *Imagined Details* vie with each other to define the evaluative context.

One such confrontation took place during the midterm meeting of Trio C-6. An essay penned by one of Ted's students was under discussion, and Laura offered a speculative point of context, an *Imagined Detail* about the student-author:

> I wonder whether . . . This student strikes me as a non-native speaker, just from . . . (C-6 Mid Trio 1515)

On the basis of his *TSK* (having known and worked with the student for five weeks), Ted flatly, and somewhat testily, rejected Laura's theory.

> *Ted:* Not at all, not at all.
> *Laura:* You don't think so?
> *Ted:* No, she is not, no. (C-6 Mid Trio 1518)

Since *TSK* as empirical knowledge usually trumps *Imagined Details* as speculative fiction, it is somewhat surprising that Laura did not immediately surrender her theory of the second-language learner. Instead, she probed further.

> *Laura:* Did her past . . . have you ever asked her what her first language is? I'm sure she speaks fluent English now.
> *Ted:* She's just so American. I haven't asked her, but I guess . . .
> *Laura:* Well, don't, you know, I'm not asking you to. (C-6 Mid Trio 1515)

This confrontation between *TSK* and *Imagined Details* appeared to end in an uneasy truce.

The end of the term found this trio in a more characteristic stand-off scenario between the two context creating techniques, in which *TSK* pushes *Imagined Details* aside in evaluative deliberations. Laura interjected an *Imagined Detail* into discussion of the portfolio submitted by one of Martin's students, and Martin gently corrected her.

> *Laura:* And actually I think he's probably an engineering student. Am I right?
> *Martin:* I don't think so.
> *Laura:* I have my little stereotypes. [LAUGHS]
> *Martin:* What is he? He's biology, that's right.
> *Laura:* Biology?
> *Martin:* Yeah. [LAUGHS] Yeah. (C-6 Port Trio 565)

Our other trio, A-1, witnessed a similar showdown. Sandra was discussing her reservations about the portfolio submitted by one of Rhonda's students. Sandra commented that one essay in the portfolio

> wasn't really a profile, and it looked to me like it was one of those kind of papers that someone sits down, you know, at twelve o'clock the night before and spends half an hour typing it up.

> *Rhonda:* Well, the sad thing is, it wasn't.
> *Sandra:* Well, it seemed like it. (A-1 Port Trio 2051)

Sandra had constructed such a strong imagined narrative of the student's skimpy writing *Effort* and *Revision* that she refused to relinquish it even when Rhonda flatly stated that in fact the student put in significant amounts of both *Effort* and *Revision* into the work presented in the portfolio.

One of the services Dynamic Criteria Mapping can provide is to document and illustrate the workings of powerful contextual criteria like *Imagined Details* and *TSK*. While the traditional response to volatile evaluative dynamics such as these is to try to expunge them from assessment procedures, my study and others (Huot 1993; Pula and Huot) suggest that these criteria are likely at work in all readings. Rather than drive them underground by insisting that instructors evaluate according to a conventional rubric, DCM can make such criteria available for discussion, negotiation, and informed policy decision. Writing programs can then publish their positions on such issues for the benefit of students and other stakeholders

Resistance to TSK and Imagined Details

By now it is obvious that *Imagined Details* and *TSK* were powerful and pervasive contextual criteria in City University's portfolio program. We have examined multiple instances of both techniques for *Constructing Writers,* and we have examined some of the evaluative complexities that they reveal. The remaining facet of *TSK* and *Imagined Details* that requires our attention is the phenomenon of resistance to both context-fabricating activities.

In the world of *Constructing Writers,* Rhonda (Trio A-1) was a quiet rebel. Believing that instructors should judge writers by their textual performances alone, she consistently challenged and obstructed efforts by her trio-mates to introduce *TSK* into trio deliberations. In the brief exchange below, Veronica asked which assignment Sandra's student's essay fulfilled. When Sandra offered a fairly pointed bit of negative *TSK* along with the basic information requested, Rhonda weighed in ironically.

> *Veronica:* Is this the significant event, this paper?
> *Sandra:* Yes, that's right, because he didn't turn in [essay] number two on time so he didn't get to make a choice.
> *Rhonda:* But don't let that influence your decision. (A-1 Mid Trio 281)

Rhonda's wry comment raised the question of why Sandra shared her negative *TSK* and whether such information should have figured into Veronica's decision-making process.

Imagined Details were also challenged, sometimes by people who frequently offered them. During the midterm meeting of Trio C-6, Laura challenged Ted's *TSK.* Not knowing at first whether Ted was the instructor of the student whose essay was under discussion, Laura opposed Ted's *TSK* because she thought Ted was instead offering *Imagined Details.* Ted had commented about one student that

> He was trying to take a free ride, I think. He's trying to get by with stuff because he just doesn't want to put the work into it.

Laura replied with some alarm,

> I think it's so dangerous to make the assumption that students like con-
> sciously or not consciously are doing something in a piece of writing. But if
> it's your student . . . (C-6 Mid Trio 1587)

Once Ted clarified that the student about whom he was talking was
indeed his own student, Laura backed off immediately. She resisted
what she thought were *Imagined Details* but—unlike Rhonda—readily
accepted *TSK*.

Norming sessions also included some protests against *Constructing
Writers*. During Team C's midterm norming, Richard resisted Sarah's
Imagined Details about the author of "Gramma Sally." As a way to explain
the stylistic and mechanical problems of "Gramma Sally," Sarah had
commented about the student-author that

> I really felt like she didn't respect her writing

Richard, however, took issue with that fictionalization.

> I don't know if it'd be fair to say that . . . this person doesn't respect their
> writing when you don't know who that was. (837)

Likewise Kevin, leader of Team C, tried to get Renee to evaluate
"Pops" "as a piece of writing" rather than on the basis of her *Imagined
Details* about the author's youth and inexperience (C Mid Norm, 1829).

Employing *TSK* and *Imagined Details*, instructors at City University frequently constructed writers to help themselves (and to help each other)
reach well-informed pass/fail decisions. Yet these two Contextual
Criteria came into conflict with each other and with objections to the
entire enterprise of author creation. Understanding these intricacies of
Constructing Writers is crucial to understanding and publicizing the evaluative topography of City University. And closely related to these two
forms of context spinning was participants' strong interest in composing a narrative of student-authors' *Learning/Progress/Growth*.

LEARNING/PROGRESS/GROWTH

Recall from chapter 3 that the Contextual criterion *Learning/Progress/
Growth* was included in the constellation *Change in Student-Author*. This
criterion acts as a portal linking the Textual and Contextual realms of
evaluative criteria in the writing program at City University. Unlike the

other two (textual) criteria in the *Change in Student-Author* constellation, *Learning/Progress/Growth* did not involve a judgment of the quality (or qualities) of a particular text or even a collection of texts. Instead, *Learning/Progress/Growth* constructed a narrative of change, momentum, and direction in an author's writing abilities as she moved from one paper to the next in the portfolio.

Discussing Portfolio #4 during Team A's end-term norming session, Terri made a comment that nicely illustrated the character of the *Learning/Progress/Growth* criterion.

> Yeah, I think if you're looking for strength in this one, if you're looking for developing strength, it's almost as if it goes the other way. The papers get WEAKER as the person moves through the quarter. And . . . that's discouraging to see that. [LAUGHTER.] That's not what we want to see in our students; regression is not what we're after. (A Port Norm 1296)

Terri touched upon the widespread hope among evaluators that portfolios would illustrate the student-author's "developing strength," and she clearly stated that when they found the opposite dynamic— writing getting progressively weaker—they felt seriously disheartened.

Note that a judgment of *Learning/Progress/Growth* was not a judgment of the rhetorical strength of the texts under consideration. Instead, *Learning* drew on differences in the relative rhetorical strengths of texts to construct an implicit narrative of the student-author's *Growth.* *Learning* was sometimes explicitly contrasted with a judgment of the quality of writing in a portfolio's contents.

In the end-term meeting of Trio A-1, for example, Sandra struggled aloud with how to make a final judgment on one of her students.

> I don't know if Brandon is a B writer or Brandon is an A writer because he was writing kind of B papers in the beginning and toward the end he started writing A papers. (A-1 Port Trio 224)

Sandra already knew how good each paper in Brandon's portfolio was. We might then expect judging the portfolio as a whole to be relatively straightforward. But because Sandra valued *Learning* distinct from the strength of each paper, she still struggled with Brandon's final grade. Veronica, Sandra's trio-mate, concurred with Sandra on this challenge: "Yeah, that makes it very difficult, actually." (A-1 Port Trio 225)

At other times, however, *Learning/Progress/Growth* appeared to help readers construct a narrative of ascent or decline that made judgment easier. In the several examples below, evaluators looked to their construction of *Learning* to point them toward either a pass or a fail decision.

> I think I would pass it, because there's improvement? (Rhonda, A-1 Port Trio, 1132)
>
> I thought portfolio four sort of went downhill on papers three and four? (Kevin, Admin Pre-Port Norm, 643)
>
> Mm-hmm. She's paying attention to audience in some ways in these last papers that she's not thinking about in the first one. (Terri, C Port Norm, 1606)
>
> And one thing that kind of bothered me, he started out . . . I think [the essay about] basketball is almost his best one in a sense, and they kind of go down. (Martin, C-6 Port Trio, 1002)

Evaluated according to the criterion *Learning/Progress/Growth*, writers who seemed to improve over the course of their time assembling the portfolio were more likely to pass. Those who appeared to go "downhill" were more likely to fail.

Yet at least one instructor problematized this stock axiological narrative through which *Learning* operated as a criterion for judgment. Halfway through discussions in portfolio norming for Team C, an adjunct named Chris offered this observation.

> A lot of the people have been saying that as they got towards the end of the portfolio . . . You know, the assumption being that they [students] should have learned, they should have gotten better and better in a sense. But also keep in mind that the assignments are getting harder, and, you know, there's just no way . . . That student may have gotten the final essay and had to work forty hours that week, you know, and didn't produce as fine a paper as they could have. I just don't think you can make an assumption automatically that the papers are going to improve . . . [that] if they're learning that those papers will get better and better. You know, because the assignments are also getting more and more difficult. I think that's just a consideration. (C Port Norm 1396)

Chris challenged the contextual criterion *Learning/Progress/Growth* by adding further layers of contextualizing narrative (in the form of admittedly speculative *Imagined Details*). Whereas *Learning* prompted confidently constructed narratives of ascent or decline (or a "flat line") in rhetorical ability based on differences or similarities among portfolio artifacts, Chris asked his colleagues to consider alternative interpretations that would mediate the impact of *Learning* as a factor for judgment.

Specifically, Chris wanted instructors to figure in the fact that English 1 assignments steadily—and appropriately—increased in difficulty. (Note that *Difficulty of the Writing Task* is a Contextual Criterion in its own right, discussed below.) Therefore a decline in writing quality might have indicated a student's difficulty meeting new rhetorical challenges rather than lack of interest, effort, or development. Somewhat more speculatively, though just as reasonably, Chris also insisted that circumstances of students' lives—such as their jobs—significantly affected their abilities to perform on English 1 assignments. Chris apparently felt uncomfortable with his colleagues' easy assumptions around *Learning/Progress/Growth* and so attempted to disrupt its smooth narrative/evaluative function.

Another intriguing aspect of *Learning/Progress/Growth* was its meta-function in relation to many other criteria, both textual and contextual. In the course of discussing how much a given student-author apparently "improved" or "dwindled," evaluators touched on these other criteria, which were the specific areas or ways in which *Progress* occurred (or failed to occur):

> *Interesting/Lively/Creative*
> *Mechanics*
> *Effort/Taking Risks*
> *Audience Awareness*
> *Ready for English 2*
> *Difficulty of the Writing Task*
> *Writing Center*
> *Authority/Take Charge/Serious*

In other words, *Learning/Progress/Growth* was a unique criterion in taking as its warrant evaluators' judgments regarding various *other* criteria.

It is also interesting to note that a portfolio did not have to "drop off" to be judged as lacking in *Learning/Progress/Growth*. "Flat line" portfolios (those that showed little change from one essay to the next) were also often judged as distinctly lacking in this area. During Team C's norming discussion of Portfolio #2, Richard illustrated this view with the following comment (Richard had voted in the minority to fail Portfolio #2 [sixteen voted to pass, five to fail]):

> [T]his person makes the same errors throughout all the papers, so it didn't seem like he or she was learning whatever needed to be done, like especially comma splices [inaudible]. And I found some of these exact same spelling

errors on the exact same kind of words in different essays. So they weren't improving their mistakes, whatever those were, and I think, you know, I'm assuming they had the chance to do that. (C Port Norm 1191)

Ralph was especially dissatisfied with "Arthurs," the final text in Portfolio #2, which he read first. After reading "Arthurs," Ralph explained,

> I jumped back and I looked at the last one to try to figure out where this pers—to look for signs of growth, or where this person was going to, or what skills this person was taking into English 2? And I went . . . I asked myself, "Do I want to be the person to send this person to English 2?" and I couldn't in all good conscience say, "Yeah, I wanna be the English 2 professor on the receiving end of this student." (C Port Norm 1220)

Portfolio #2 suffered in Ralph's estimation specifically because, in his reading, it showed no signs of improvement from essay to essay. Thus, the absence of evidence pointing to *Learning/Progress/Growth* functions evaluatively much in the same way as direct evidence of decline. (More discussion of the distinct Contextual Criterion *Ready for English 2* appears below.)

A final note on this criterion came from Ted during the end-term meeting of Trio C-6. Under his scrutiny, Ted explained, students profited from either the presence or absence of *Learning/Progress/Growth*.

> I try to be real win-win about this. If they start off badly and they develop well, that's good and then I think they can make it. If they start off well and then don't do very well later, well at one time they could and that means that they can. (Ted, C-6 Port Trio 2289)

In Ted's distinctive case, students benefited either way. Both ascent and decline were interpreted favorably and pointed toward a "pass" decision.

"SHALL I UTTER THE DREAD WORD?": PLAGIARISM AND ORIGINALITY

Scholarship in rhetoric on the topics of plagiarism, "recycling," "sampling," and other issues of intellectual property has been especially lively in recent years. In this context, City University's instructors provided stimulating examples of how such issues played out in evaluating students' rhetorical performances.

As with all Contextual Criteria, it is useful to be reminded that *Plagiarism/Originality* has nothing to do with the quality of the textual performance presented for judgment. It matters little, in other words, how "good" a student's essay is if it was downloaded from the World Wide Web, copied from the encyclopedia or a scholarly journal, or submitted for credit in a previous course. *Plagiarism/Originality* as a rhetorical value points to our implicit expectations that each student- author will do the intellectual, artistic, and physical work of fulfilling writing assignments and always carefully document any material drawn from other sources.

Participants in my study occasionally suspected that writing they were evaluating had been plagiarized. The most discussed example was the "profile" essay ("What Is NSBE") in Portfolio #4. In Team A's end-term norming discussion, Terri introduced the topic by commenting that

> a lot of that sounded to me as if it was taken directly from some materials . . . that the person had, some kind of brochure. . . . I think that she lifted a lot of that material. You can just pick out, sentence by sentence, what's her own and . . . so it has this odd quality, and you feel really turned around as a reader. From the sort of inept sentences to the ones that are clearly lifted from someplace else. (Terri, A Port Norm 1341)

Based on her analysis of stylistic inconsistencies within that single essay, Terri (along with many other program instructors) concluded that in her essay the student had presented text that came from another source without documenting that source or flagging the borrowed text.

While the essay "What Is NSBE" in Portfolio #4 came under suspicion due to its internal stylistic clashes, plagiarism might also be suspected because of inconsistencies among essays in a portfolio. At the end of the term, an adjunct named Charlotte shared with her colleagues on Team A a troubling situation that had arisen in her classroom. In response to her colleagues' discussion of how the in-class essay functioned for them as "a gauge to make sure that the student hasn't been getting their essays somewhere else," Charlotte described her predicament.

> This one in-class essay by the student was just atrocious and the first three papers were, you know, B, and so I haven't quite addressed how to handle it once the person [INAUDIBLE] . . . I'm really wondering if this person is bringing [INAUDIBLE], so . . . It's SERIOUSLY problematic. (A Port Norm 1163)

(See the next section for discussion of how participants gauged the relative importance of the in-class essay and the revised writing in portfolios.) Not surprisingly, many instructors shared Charlotte's sense of profound unease when faced with possible plagiarism. In response to Andrea's mock-dramatic question "Shall I actually utter the dread word 'plagiarism'?" for example, Terri went out of her way to explain that she saw the author of Portfolio #4 as unaware of her plagiarism.

> I don't think this is a deliberate attempt to plagiarize in any kind of malicious sense. . . . I think this person is just sort of desperately trying to write this paper and gathering whatever information she can find, and feels like, you know, "Well, I can't say it any better than that," so she jots it down. . . . I think you would have to speak to this person about plagiarism. (A Port Norm 1071)

By assuming the student's lack of awareness of, and therefore of bad motive for, the act of plagiarism, Terri defuses some of the ethical tension from the pedagogical and evaluative scenario and opens a way for a teacher to address and educate the student on the ethical and rhetorical issues involved in plagiarism.

Instructors also grappled with some thorny theoretical issues surrounding the question of plagiarism, originality, and style. During Team C's portfolio norming session, three instructors explored and debated the meaning and significance of the very close similarity between the opening line of Portfolio #3's essay "Professional Helper" and an essay entitled "Soup" from the course text (Axelrod and Cooper, 100). Jennifer was the first person to notice the similarity.

> *Jennifer:* I also felt that the opening of the "Professional Helper" was an awful lot like the opening of the essay "Soup" that we read this week. (Jennifer, C Port Norm 1774)

Jennifer's colleagues were quick to recognize and agree with her observation.

VIDEO NOTE: [6]
[Laura smiles at Jennifer. Terri nods her head thoughtfully. Others leaf
   through their portfolio guides to look at "Professional Helper."]
Various Voices: Yeah. Hmmm. Yeah, that's true.
Mike: Busted.
Martin: "Baseball is my life." Yeah, that is true.
Unidentified woman: Hmmm. Oh wow. That is.
Ralph: Hmmm. I didn't notice that. (C Port Norm 1785)

After a few more minutes of discussion, Ted weighed in with some critical questions about the group's sense that the author of "Professional

Helper" may have done something illicit, something for which he should be "busted."

> *Ted:* I have a question. You said that this was a lot like "Soup." I have kind of an inkling as to why that might be a problem, but I'd like to hear explicitly: why is that a problem? This is not . . . that's not plagiarism when you take a form and re-apply it. That's how—that's the way we used to teach writing . . .
> *Terri:* Models.
> *Ted:* Why is that bad? (C Port Norm 1839)

Jennifer tries to explain why the similarity disturbed her.

> I think I reacted negatively to it because it was very, very similar. . . . I don't want them to use exact sentence structure and phrasing just like some of the things we've read, or that they've read. (C Port Norm 1842)

For Jennifer, then, "exact sentence structure and phrasing" crossed the line from rhetorical or literary "modeling" to plagiarism. But Martin, an aficionado of baseball journalism, had yet another perspective to offer on the question of plagiarism in "Professional Helper."

> *Martin:* Well, one thing that's kind of weird, but—not just "Soup," but I mean if you read an article about Pete Rose, a lot of times you'll see "Pete Rose says, 'Baseball is my life'" or "Roy Hobbs says, 'Baseball is my life.'"
> *Terri:* Cliché. [laughs]
> *Martin:* Yeah, I mean that's a standard way a lot of people who're paid to write stuff about baseball start it out. (C Port Norm 1858)

Jennifer raised the question of plagiarism; Ted questioned the line dividing it from modeling; and Martin highlighted the relevance of journalistic conventions or clichés. Even in this single, relatively brief exchange, we can see the complexities of judging *Plagiarism/Originality* proliferating.

"IN THE CONTEXT OF THE ENTIRE PORTFOLIO IT'S PRETTY CLEAR": PORTFOLIO VS. ESSAY EVALUATION

This entire chapter is devoted to exploring how different contexts for students' writing influenced instructors' judgments in City University's portfolio program. We've looked at how program standards, constructions of writers, narratives of growth, and suspicions of plagiarism shaped those decisions. Ironically, we might risk overlooking that one of the prime motives for using portfolios as opposed to lone essays has always been to provide a richer context for—and thereby enhance the validity of—high-stakes decisions about students' writing abilities. Portfolios are, in and of themselves, powerful contexts for rhetorical judgment. The discourse of participants in this study lays out several specific ways in which evaluation of portfolios differs from evaluations of single texts.

The clearest articulation of the overall distinction between essay and portfolio assessment came from Terri during the administrators' meeting to prepare for end-term norming sessions. All three administrators agreed that Portfolio #3 should fail. Emily, FYE Program director, then asked Kevin and Terri to discuss how they should respond to instructors who might want to pass Portfolio #3. Terri observed,

> Well, if it were just that paper ["Cheers"] we'd be having a different reaction if we were just dealing with that single essay. . . . But as part of the whole portfolio, we have to take the whole portfolio into account, I don't think I can pass it because it's part of the portfolio of other work that isn't passing for me. (Admin Pre-Port Norm 971)

During Team A's end-term norming session, an adjunct named Ben made a similar comment during his struggle to see Portfolio #2 as passing.

> I think that would be true [Portfolio #2 would pass] if we had one or two papers, but a portfolio is a collection, and I think that's a different kind of story. . . . It just squeaks by. Individual papers I wouldn't have trouble passing. (Ben, A Port Norm 898)

Both Terri's and Ben's remarks show that judging an essay in the context of a portfolio is significantly different from judging that essay alone.

One way in which this difference worked was that instructors didn't want to pass students based on only one good essay. In response to his peers' enthusiasm during Team C midterm norming for aspects of "Gramma Sally," Peter complained,

> [O]n the basis of one interesting essay, I don't think they should be passing the course. Too many problems. (C Mid Norm 865)

Peter believed that this student-author was simply lucky enough "to have an interesting story to tell." Doubting the writer's basic skills, Peter would insist on seeing more than one lively essay to pass the student for the course.

The reverse was also true: administrators and instructors felt that one bad essay shouldn't cause an entire portfolio to fail. For example, several members of Team C judged one of the essays from Portfolio #1 "terrible," yet they voted to pass the portfolio. Terri commented,

> If you remember our first portfolio, which was, you know, clearly hands-down passing, had one terrible paper in it. . . . The problem-solution paper in there was just awful. So that's why we look at this holistically. One paper is not gonna drag the portfolio down or up. It is a holistic assessment that we're doing; we're looking at the whole thing. (C Port Norm 2077)

Which is not to say that a single essay might not tip the scales one way or another on a borderline portfolio, as was the case for Laura when she evaluated Portfolio #2:

> "Arthurs". . . I wouldn't have failed it until I read "Arthurs." (C Port Norm 1323)

In interviews, Program Director Emily articulated two additional advantages of judging students according to their entire portfolios: one was safety, the other, quality and quantity of evidence on which the decision would be based.

> [I]n the portfolio we will see the student in several modes, we'll see several kinds of successes and certain kinds of failures, we'll get a clear sense of patterns. So, I think that student is safer when we look at several pieces.
> [S]o there are different ways to tell the story or to read the evidence here, and people construct different stories. I think, then, you make your judgment more on the basis of fact. . . . [I]t seemed to me that this is much easier, that we just have much more evidence. (Emily 1, 182)

Emily viewed portfolio evaluation as safer for the student, and she felt it provided a more valid warrant for high-stakes decisions because it offered better evidence and more facts. Interestingly, these two advantages to portfolio assessment combined for Emily into yet another difference between judging single texts and judging collections. She believed that portfolios allow evaluators to see the student-author's "whole person" by providing access to their "story" as a writer.

> I think with the portfolio, we begin to have a story of someone's progress. . . . So that now you're making much more a judgment of a person's progress rather than a judgment of the single [essay]. (Emily 3, 84, 100)

By contrast, when the program previously judged students' rhetorical competence on the basis of a single essay (a timed impromptu effort), it was forced to focus on an object rather than a person.

> When you graded single papers in an exit exam . . . you weren't really look-ing at a student, his development, you weren't looking at the story of some-body, you were just looking at this object. (Emily 3, 85)

Emily made the most sweeping and most fully theorized claims for a sub-stantial theme in the program: that judging single essays differed signifi-cantly from judging portfolios. The difference was the richness of rhetorical and evaluative *context* the portfolios provided.

"ON THE RECEIVING END OF THIS STUDENT": READY FOR ENGLISH 2

To assist them in resolving ambiguous or contentious judgments, par-ticipants often looked to English 2 (the second course in the FYE Program sequence) for guidance and clarification. Sometimes the con-textual criterion *Ready for English 2* appeared to function as a plea for "higher" standards, which suggests a close evaluative link to the crite-rion *Standards/Expectations*. During Team A's midterm norming, for example, Terri asked the group

> [D]o we want them to pass on to English 2 with this skill level? Probably not. (A Mid Norm 1134)

At the end of the term, TA Edwina voiced a parallel concern:

> [L]et's give kids more work where they need it. Let's not get 'em into English 2 where now they're really in desperate shape and they're floundering because the ideas are so difficult to grapple with and they still haven't kind of gotten the basic. I felt like this writer was like on the edge. (A Port Norm 722)

And Ben commented about the student-author of sample Portfolio # 2,

> I would hate to run into this student with that second paper in English 2 right off the bat, though. [LAUGHS] (A Port Norm 857)

Like these comments from Terri, Edwina, and Ben, most appeals to this criterion motivated participants toward failing rather than passing students' texts. *Ready for English 2* can therefore properly be understood partly as a standard-booster.

However, other, more complex dynamics were also at play here. Rather than pointing to the generally "higher" standards to which students would be held in the course English 2, some participants named specific intellectual and rhetorical skills students needed to demonstrate in English 1 in order to be ready to move on through the First-Year English sequence.

Explaining why she found the essay "Arthurs" "the weakest one" in Portfolio #2, Rhonda pointed to the author's failure to integrate her "field notes" (raw observational data) into the discussion and analysis of the restaurant under review.

> [I]t's not really incorporated into the text, it's just sort of stuck there. (A Port Norm 663)

In the next moment, however, Rhonda explained that the student's inability to weave data into an argument was not, she believed, an appropriate reason to fail the portfolio, because

> that's something that English 2 would be working on . . . so I didn't think the other thing justified not passing English 1. (A Port Norm 672)

Rhonda did not want this English 1 student to be evaluated according to skills she would be subsequently taught in English 2. So Rhonda's appeal to the criterion *Ready for English 2* was an argument to pass, rather than fail, this sample text.

Contrary to Rhonda's view, John (TA on Team C) felt that precisely because English 2 attends more to "analysis," the author of sample Portfolio #4 should fail because she showed little ability to analyze a subject.

> [T]he more we went into analysis and that sort of thing, the worse it got. I don't think this is a person who would be ready for English 2 at all. (C Port Norm 1025)

To John's critique of Portfolio #4, Terri added concerns for "organizational skills," again with specific reference to the author's being "a person we cannot let go on to English 2."

In their end-term meeting, Trio C-6 added "ability to present a clear argument" and "he doesn't lose himself" to the list of writing abilities that English 2 requires. They also showed that they viewed the later papers in the English 1 portfolio as a transition into the assignments and demands of English 2. Martin, arguing to fail a portfolio written by one of Ted's students, explained,

> the last two are the ones, the biggest sort of links to English 2, and that's what she did the worst. (C-6 Port Trio 2280)

Their trio-mate Laura concurred:

> [Y]ou're questioning critical thinking skills that she needs to go into English 2 and I have to agree with you that tends to be where she falls apart. (C-6 Port Trio 2323)

In an interview, Rhonda (from Trio A-1) offered a similar conception of how the assignments and rhetorical skills of English 1 relate to English 2 and, therefore, to the summative judgment of English 1 portfolios. Reflecting on one of her own students whose work Rhonda judged more critically than did her trio-mates, Rhonda explained that she was

> thinking how she's going to do in English 2, because her strength is as a narrative writer. (Rhonda 490)

Though her student wrote good narratives early in the quarter, her inability to analyze and evaluate in later assignments caused Rhonda to doubt the student's readiness to proceed to English 2. Ted added a useful dimension to the phenomenon of imagining students in English 2. At the time of my second interview with him, he was actually teaching English 2, and in his section of that course was enrolled one of his students from English 1. Ted had thought this student should fail English 1, but his trio-mates Laura and Martin persuaded him to pass the student.

> [A]s it turns out, he should have failed; I was right he should have failed. I've got him now, he's just really having a hard time. (Ted 2, 164)

Dynamic Criteria Mapping reveals that evaluators imagined students and instructors in English 2 to help them decide whether to pass or fail students' English 1 portfolios. If English 2 instructors like Ted could also communicate to evaluators the validity of their pass/fail decisions for English 1 students, the English 2 instructors could help validate and adjust the evaluative framework used at the conclusion of English 1. Evaluative connections between the two courses should not, in other words, be left solely to speculation, as they mainly were at City University.

Instructors sometimes attempted to project imaginatively into the English 2 classroom, to imagine a particular student there and especially to imagine themselves or one of their colleagues teaching that student. During Team C's portfolio norming session, Ralph reported that

> I asked myself, "Do I want to be the person to send this person to English 2?" and I couldn't in all good conscience say, "Yeah, I wanna be the English 2 professor on the receiving end of this student." (C Port Norm 1224)

Ralph's response to this imaginative exercise was to vote to fail sample Portfolio #2, which the administrative leaders had agreed should pass.

Links between English 1 and English 2 provided substantial and complex points of reference for evaluators trying to decide whether students were "proficient" in college writing and therefore qualified to proceed with the FYE Program sequence and their college careers. *Ready for English 2* could be a rallying cry to raise expectations, to focus on some criteria more than others, or to project imaginatively into the situation of learning and teaching the next course in the sequence.

"ARE WE DOING HER A FAVOR?": BENEFIT TO STUDENT

Another way in which evaluators looked outside of a student's text(s) to reach a pass/fail decision was to focus on what would be best for that student. Unfortunately, analyses of what decision provided the most *Benefit to Student* pointed in a variety of directions and did not always ease the challenge of reaching a judgment, whether individually or collectively.

We might expect *Benefit to Student* to motivate toward passing a student rather than failing. Sometimes it did.

> [M]aybe I should pass it. Because I think he should be given the benefit of the doubt, not me. Know what I mean? (Veronica, A-1 Port Trio, 2191)

Much more often, however, *Benefit to Student* actually pointed evaluators towards failing students.

> [F]or the purpose of this course, it's not going to serve the writer well to support this kind of writing. I mean if they turn this in in engineering or nursing school, they're going to have a problem. So, you know, to serve this student, as far as what the ends of the course are, I don't think it would be serving their needs to be supportive of this kind of writing in this context. (Renee, C Mid Norm 1505)

[T]he student's interests wouldn't be served by passing her at this point; that
we wouldn't be doing her a favor . . . by depriving her of the kind of instruction that we're supposed to be giving to students. (Kevin 1, 34)

I mean, I'm worried. Are we doing her a favor by passing her? . . . I don't
know if it'd be better [for her] to repeat English 1 if—I really don't think
she'd pass English 2. (Martin, C-6 Port Trio 2041)

[W]hen it gets to borderline, then what we need to look at in terms of doing
the student a favor . . . I saw a real drop-off at the end there. She may need
another quarter [of English 1]. (Laura, C-6 Port Trio 2246)

Kevin and Laura saw struggling students as entitled to additional
instructional resources; Renee and Martin worried that such students
would be set up for failure if they proceeded to English 2 and to various
majors across the university. Both kinds of concerns for students' best
interests inclined these instructors toward failing borderline students.

In my first interview with Terri, she nicely summed up the complexities of "compassion" in teaching and assessing composition. Describing
her initial responses to the sample text "Gramma Sally," Terri explained,

I tend to be more compassionate probably than is good for my students and
so I know that I have to watch myself. (Terri 1, 141)

Seeing the great potential in "Gramma Sally," she would want to encourage the student and send her to the Writing Center for help. She might,
then, be tempted to pass the essay against her better judgment.

I tend to give her the benefit of the doubt where it really doesn't serve the
purposes of this program to do that. (Terri 1, 141)

Wanting the best for her students, Terri would feel compassion for them
and a desire to help and support them. Ironically, she saw these feelings
as ultimately working directly against the students' best interests, as well
as against those of the FYE Program. Thus Terri found herself stuck in a
conundrum of compassion.

"WHAT'S THE FUNCTION OF THIS CLASS WE'RE TEACHING?": GOALS FOR ENGLISH 1

Most of participants' discussion of *Goals for English 1* as a Contextual
Criterion for judging students focused on the sample text "Anguish."
That text was widely regarded as employing a discourse or dialect other
than what Kevin called "public discourse . . . or academic discourse."

Some instructors also constructed the author of "Anguish" as African American in ethnicity.

Instructors agreed that "Anguish" had merit of different kinds but debated whether it was passing work for English 1 because of its alien discourse, most evident to instructors in the essay's frequent shifts between present and past tenses. TA Renee took the lead in explaining her critique of this sample essay to Team C:

> [R]eally what we're trying to do is introduce these students to the quote-unquote "normal discourse"? That's gonna be expected of them in the academic environment . . . And this is not it. You know. I mean, this could be in another setting something wonderful to work with, but for what we're—for the purpose of this course, it's not going to serve the writer well to support this kind of writing. (C Mid Norm 1497)

About a minute later, Linda added another perspective to questions about whether "Anguish" met the goals of the course. For her, the key goal for English 1 was for students to learn to trace "cause and effect" in their essays.

> Ultimately we're teaching them how to write in other fields about cause and effect . . . ultimately the papers that have come back that I felt were really strong essays were addressing that, even if they weren't aware that they were addressing that. And with this "Anguish" paper, I feel like . . . I'm a little disturbed at what I'm hearing in that . . . This is probably a very fine piece of creative non-fiction and this movement of tenses I think I agree with Ted is what really moves it along and makes it strong, and I'm hearing people . . . maybe we're going to discourage this person from some of the strengths of her writing because she experiments with tenses. That kind of disturbs me. But I would not be able to pass it because it does not ultimately fulfill the criteria of an essay. (C Mid Norm 1547)

Despite her careful attention to and strong agreement with Ted's arguments on behalf of passing "Anguish" for its compelling "literary" qualities as a "scream" of grief, Linda voted to fail the essay because she found its exposition of cause and effect confused.

In my first interview with Veronica, however, she presented a different view of the essential features of English 1 as an introductory course in college composition:

> In my own personal experiences, I mean [English 1 is] the one course where a student is exploring who they are as a writer and what that identity is beginning

to feel [like] to them. You know, like what it's beginning to mean . . . I really mean this very seriously. (Veronica 1, 133)

Depending on their deeply felt sense of what were the core goals of English 1, instructors might pass or fail an essay like "Anguish" or Portfolio #4 (both authored by students that readers constructed as African American).

"POINTS FOR TAKING ON A TOUGHER TASK": DIFFICULTY OF THE WRITING TASK

Participants sometimes guided their evaluations by how challenging a rhetorical task the student and her text took on. Discussing "Gramma Sally" in Team C's midterm norming session, Ted took an unusual position on the question of *Difficulty of the Writing Task:*

> I do remember thinking that "Pops" was not quite the challenge that some of the other essays were. But I don't feel like I need to give points for taking on a tougher task. The point is whether you've written a good essay. (C Mid Norm 784)

Ted did not want to figure in how challenging a topic or rhetorical task the author had taken on; he wanted to limit his judgments to the effectiveness of the final product.

Most instructors who commented on *Difficulty* disagreed with Ted. From the TA named Mike, the author of "Gramma Sally" received credit for doing a mixed job on a very tough topic, while the author of "Belle" (one of only two sample texts passed by every instructor in the program) fell in his esteem because the topic was intellectually and emotionally easy to handle.

> It just impressed me that ["Gramma Sally"] was a sort of sophisticated thing to have to grapple with, and sort of a hard subject. In that "Belle" was really well written, but was just about some grand old gal, you know? (Mike, C Mid Norm 385)

At the end of the term, however, Mike was more critical than most instructors of Portfolio #2, especially the essay "Arthurs." Because Terri felt that "Arthurs" tackled an unusual challenge—integrating interview material into the restaurant review—she challenged Mike to consider how tough a challenge the author had taken up.

This is a pretty sticky formal problem. I thought: I don't know exactly how I would do this. This is quite a task, to figure out how to organize this material. And if you were going to be correct, to have it all in quotes, Mike, how would you do it? (Terri, C Port Norm 1495)

Difficulty of the Writing Task seems to be related to the textual criterion *Effort/Taking Risks*. The distinction between them is whether the special effort or risk taking lies more in the nature of the task set for or chosen by the author (Contextual *Difficulty*) or in the author's execution of the task (Textual *Effort/Taking Risks*).

"I ASSIGNED HIM TO GO GET HELP": THE WRITING CENTER

The Writing Center at City University was located right there on the third floor of Hancock Hall alongside FYE Program and English department classrooms and offices. Though references to *The Writing Center* were relatively modest in number, this contextual criterion had special power of two kinds. First, it figured quite prominently in the reasoning behind judgments of certain texts. Also, there appeared to be a significant gap between many instructors' assumptions about the Writing Center as a resource supporting students and its actual availability to student-writers. Material revealed on this topic by Dynamic Criteria Mapping provides an opportunity to consider how a program's writing center functions in students' writing processes and how considerations of those facts should figure into evaluations of students' textual performances.

Right or wrong, many instructors held an almost magical faith in the capacity of the Writing Center to cure student-authors of their rhetorical ills.

[A]nother thing about this person is that the problems that they have might . . . be easily addressed in a writing center conference or two. (Terri, A Mid Norm 1010)

And if she is having these problems, the Writing Center could straighten them out. (Linda, C Mid Norm 1114)

I assigned him to go get help from the writing center. (Martin, C-6 Mid Trio 1310)

I looked at that paper and I would think: God, you know, if I had this for ten minutes in the writing center this would be a great paper. I mean not just a passing paper but it could be a really fine paper if I just had this person for a few minutes, you know. (Terri 1, 144)

The common evaluative implication of this faith in the Writing Center was that borderline texts failed because instructors believed authors could have gone the Writing Center to get help with their problems. If texts that came before them for evaluation showed difficulties of various kinds (most often with *Mechanics*), students were assumed to have neglected to make use of the Writing Center as a resource.

What many instructors were apparently unaware of was that in the academic year in which I collected my data, City University Writing Center staffing had been curtailed due to budget cuts. As a result, according to several sources with whom I spoke, the average waiting period for getting help at the Writing Center was two weeks. This meant that between the time an English 1 essay was assigned and the time it was due to the instructor, a student might not be able to get help from the Writing Center at all.

OTHER CONTEXTUAL CRITERIA

Approximately ten contextual criteria remain to be discussed; because they are relatively minor quantitatively, I will touch on them only briefly here before concluding this chapter.

Fairness and Hypocrisy

Two instructors, Veronica and Ted, discussed situations they felt were unfair or hypocritical. Veronica thought her peers' demand that students from different cultural and linguistic backgrounds "cross over" into academic discourse was hypocritical because the academics refused to do the same.

> [W]e were failing the student for not making a cultural transition and we're totally incapable of making it ourselves. To me that doesn't seem fair. (Veronica 1, 59)

> On the one hand we are encouraging creativity, that's sort of [INAUDIBLE] but on the other hand we want it curtailed. (Veronica 2, 474)

On a similar track, Ted was quite agitated that he couldn't get Kevin, associate director of FYE and professor/leader of Team C, to understand or accept the concerns that led Ted to argue, passionately and at length, for passing the sample text "Anguish."

> I'm feeling uncomfortable that we tell [students] one thing and grade them on another way. I say, "Give me voice, give me fire," and then when I get it I flunk it. I don't think that's right. (Ted 1, 451)

Writer Shows Promise

In a dynamic closely parallel to that of *Benefit to Student,* the criterion *Writer Shows Promise* occasionally worked in a student's favor but more often counted against that student.

> I see . . . potential for this person. (Pat, C Mid Norm 369)

> You know it's funny, Laura, because I would have an easier time flunking it for the very reasons you're saying, because I think this person could be a really good writer. But she doesn't respect her writing? (Sarah, C Mid Norm 806)

> I think that the author does show some of the promise that you discussed. I'm concerned, though . . . (Laura, C Port Norm 1265)

> Kevin would say: But hey, you know, this is the state it's in right now and we have to deal with the state it's in right now. I tend to be swayed by somebody's potential, and in some ways Kevin is able to talk me out of that. (Terri 1, 160)

It would be helpful not only to students but also to writing instructors to be alerted that criteria like *Writer Shows Promise* that seem to favor students may, in practice, count against them.

Cultural Differences

Veronica was the only participant to raise *Cultural Differences* as an evaluative concern. This criterion was closely connected to the issues she raised above under *Fairness/Hypocrisy.* The following quotation aptly summarizes Veronica's view of how *Cultural Differences* functioned in the program.

> Because I think we are not even accounting for the fact that this person [the author of the sample essay "Anguish"] may have a different approach to telling a good story as opposed to what we might have and we think it's some kind of error or some kind of exposure and I think it may be true that this person has not written a lot and that does not mean he is not capable of writing better next quarter. (Veronica 1, 67)

Using the Spell Check

Two participants in Team C portfolio norming mentioned the use of computerized spell checkers in discussing their judgments of sample portfolios. Chris counted against the author of Portfolio #4 the fact that she apparently had not run a spell check even though she was writing in a computer classroom (as evidenced by the in-class essay being in typescript rather than manuscript):

Just out of curiosity . . . This was one of those computer classes. . . . Do they use spell checks? . . . Some of it [the portfolio's spelling problems] was they were using the wrong word, but then some of it was unexplainable. (C Port Norm 1082)

Martin, on the other hand, came to the aid of the author of Portfolio #3 and the essay "Professional Helper" by observing that a misspelling many of his fellow instructors had criticized (the name of the baseball player featured in the essay) was a misspelling with which a computer could not help.

I mean, yeah, he [misspelled] the name . . . the spelling with the name . . . But gosh, I mean, it's something . . . the spell-checker's not going to pick that up, so I gave him a little leeway there. (C Port Norm 1755)

Through mapping this Contextual Criterion, we learn that the use or neglect of spell checkers receives evaluators' attention and that the *Using the Spell Check* can work for or against the student-author.

Constructing Teachers

During the midterm meeting of Trio C-6, Ted revealed his ongoing development as an English 1 instructor and how he thought his professional evolution should figure into the trio's judgment of a particular paper.

[T]his was the first paper; it was not until the beginning of this week that I began to get clear on exactly what the expectations were of this class. So, I don't think that's a failing paper. (C-6 Mid Trio 1456)

Ted points toward a potentially volatile but also highly relevant and powerful Contextual Criterion rarely addressed in discussions of writing assessment: how the professional growth and awareness (or mood or level of exhaustion) of the instructor-evaluator shapes evaluation. Having been brought to our attention through DCM, this criterion deserves further investigation and discussion.

Compassion for Writer

As with several other criteria that suggest they might motivate toward passing rather than failing students' texts, in the two instances in which it was explicitly mentioned, *Compassion for Writer* turned out not to help students. In Team C's end-term norming session, TA Leslie exclaimed about Portfolio #4,

> It was tearing my heart out to read this portfolio, oh my God this poor girl! I
> felt so bad. (C Port Norm 860)

Though she didn't explicate, Leslie's anguished empathy appears to be
for the author's struggles with writing rather than with the circumstances
of her life. Notably, however, Leslie's compassion did not lead her to pass
Portfolio #4. In fact, every member of Team C failed that sample text.

In my first interview with Terri, she invoked the other instance of
Compassion for Writer. Here again, however, her feelings of compassion
did not lead her to favor students. On the contrary, it was an emotional
response against which she was consciously working.

> I tend to be more compassionate probably than is good for my students and
> so I know that I have to watch myself. . . . I tend to give her the benefit of the
> doubt where it really doesn't serve the purposes of this program to do that.
> (Terri 1, 141)

Instructor-evaluators felt *Compassion for Writers,* but those feelings did
not lead them to pass those writers' texts.

Time

Participants' constant concern for *Time* did not appear directly to
motivate them toward failing or passing decisions on specific texts. *Time*
did, however, shape and curtail evaluative deliberations among judges
and, therefore, likely had some impact on their decisions. Near the end
of the lengthy midterm meeting of Trio C-6, Laura initiated a new line
of inquiry with her trio-mate Ted. However, she apologized for doing so.

> But I want . . . if you have a moment, and I know that it's taking forever. Just
> so I feel like I'm getting something . . . (C-6 Mid Trio 1940)

Laura's concern for her trio-mates' (and her own) time did not prevent
her from taking up a new line of conversation, but she was nevertheless
conscious of time and apologetic for using more of it.

Discussing the community building and professional development
provided to participants in the FYE Portfolio Program, Director Emily
nevertheless noted her general reluctance to ask adjunct instructors to
invest time in such activities.

> I think the situation of the adjunct instructors here is so dismal, I mean their
> pay and working conditions, that I think that's an enormous impediment to

building a community. I think it's impossible, almost impossible for us to ask adjuncts to meet with us, to give us extra time. (Emily 3, 246)

As an administrator, Emily is torn between respecting adjuncts' time and woeful working conditions on the one hand and, on the other hand, inviting (or requiring) them to join a highly rewarding professional process.

In my interview with Rhonda, she frankly admitted that some of her comments during norming sessions were designed to bring the evaluative deliberations to a close. Though she was usually reticent during norming, she observed about one comment that

I was just surprised this time I spoke up, and partly it was because of watching the clock, I have to get out of here, I have to get out of here, so let's move this along. (Rhonda, 201)

Time operated obliquely to shape and constrain FYE instructors' and administrators' conversations. Though their impact on specific decisions is murky, time constraints must be counted as significant criterion for judgment in the program.

Turned in Late and Attendance

These last two Contextual Criteria were mentioned only briefly during discussions in the portfolio program. Martin mentioned on two occasions that his judgment of a student's text was partly influenced by the fact that the paper was *Turned In Late*. Martin was also the prime voice on Team C for figuring *Attendance* into pass/fail decisions on portfolios. But on this criterion Sandra, from Team A, joined in.

Actually it's funny, because I may not pass him anyway because he missed so many classes and stuff like that. It's just something I'm going to have to work out. (A-1 Port Trio 893)

Though minor in impact, these criteria were at work and made a significant difference to the particular students whose work was judged by them.

The Contextual Criteria explored in this chapter represent mainly uncharted territory in the study of rhetorical judgment. Since evaluative deliberations are clearly based on not only textual but also contextual considerations, any effort to tell the truth of assessment in a writing program must include mapping or charting of both realms and of their interrelationships.

We have uncovered the detailed dynamics of setting *Standards/Expectations,* mapped the multifaceted processes of *Constructing Writers,* and traced a number of other potent Contextual Criteria. Combining these analyses with findings on Textual Criteria presented in chapter 3, we emerge with a detailed, data-driven, complex, and instructive map of the axiological terrain of City University's portfolio assessment program. In my final chapter I foreground the multiple benefits of Dynamic Criteria Mapping and lay out specific strategies by which writing programs can tap into the epistemological, educational, ethical, and political power of DCM.

5

A MODEL FOR DYNAMIC CRITERIA MAPPING OF COMMUNAL WRITING ASSESSMENT

At the outset of this book, I argued that contemporary writing assessment stands in urgent need of a rigorous method for discovering how instructors of composition judge their students' work. Chapter 2 explains the context and methods for my Dynamic Criteria Mapping (DCM) project, and chapters 3 and 4 detail what I learned from using DCM in my study of City University. At the outset of this concluding chapter I foreground the benefits of DCM for all college and university writing programs and for other organizations. I end by proposing specific strategies by which writing programs can employ this method for investigation, negotiation, and publication of their rhetorical values. In light of the substantial educational, ethical, and political benefits provided by DCM, the additional investment of time and energy required to conduct serious axiological inquiry is surprisingly and encouragingly modest.

When compositionists inevitably encounter obstacles and pressures motivating against such additional investment of resources, I hope they will focus on their students. For while faculty, programs, and others benefit significantly from DCM, it is our students who most urgently lack what DCM offers. Because they possess no adequate account of how their work is evaluated, they cannot do two important things: 1) understand the dynamics by which their rhetorical efforts are evaluated across the writing program and hold their instructors and administrators accountable for those dynamics, and 2) work from a detailed, nuanced representation of evaluative dynamics to enhance their long-term development and their immediate success as rhetors

In my experience conducting on-site DCM with several groups of faculty (and in listening to reviewers of this book), it is clear that DCM transforms the way we understand not only writing assessment but the nature of composition itself. DCM reveals and highlights the complex, conflicted, communal quilt of rhetorical values that any group of composition instructors inevitably creates in the very act of teaching and assessing writing together. For all these reasons, students and teachers of writing need the truth about writing assessment. It is our responsibility to help them discover, compose, revise, and publish that truth.

BENEFITS OF DCM: RETURNS ON THE INVESTMENT

For writing programs that already conduct communal writing assessment along the lines of City University's or SUNY Stonybrook's, the additional resources—and the conceptual changes—required to carry out DCM should be relatively modest. However, obstacles to DCM will appear. For starters, any significant change in practices of teaching and assessment will require exceptional dedication and perseverance by faculty and administrators simply to overcome the inertia of how things have "always" been done. Furthermore, in our contemporary social context, educational resources are chronically scarce. While some sectors of our economy reap record profits year after year, schools, colleges, and universities must scrape and beg for what they need to prepare students for participation in democratic society. In light of these likely barriers to implementing the practices I propose below, I first want to highlight the benefits that make Dynamic Criteria Mapping worth the additional investment it requires of writing programs, colleges, and universities— and of the publics that support them.

1. Student Learning. At the heart of what we do is the student, striving to learn and succeed. Learning to write well is clearly one of the most powerful elements in any person's potential for success in personal life, professional life, and democratic citizenship. I believe in the unparalleled educational potential for Dynamic Criteria Mapping to give our students a more complex and more true portrait of how writing is learned, practiced, and valued. The author of the sample essay "Pops," for example, could likely make excellent use of the criterion *Empty/ Hollow/Clichéd,* on the basis of which one in ten writing faculty failed her essay. Likewise the author of "Gramma Sally" could take heart from knowing that her essay accomplished some of the most highly valued rhetorical goals in the program—*Significance, Interesting, Sincerity,* and *Taking Risks*—while also understanding that half the instructors failed her for significant and repeated faults in *Mechanics, Control,* and *Consistency.* Equipped with such knowledge, students will better understand the challenge of writing well and will have more and better information about how to succeed in the effort. Exploring students' perspectives on DCM will also, I believe, prove a fascinating and productive topic of future research in the field of writing assessment.

2. *Professional Development and Community.* Communal writing assessment, and especially Dynamic Criteria Mapping, require more of faculty than do teaching and grading in isolation. Fortunately, DCM also offers tremendous potential for writing instructors' professional growth and feeling of professional community. As Belanoff and Elbow (1991) and I (1994a; 1997; 2000) have argued, participation in communal writing assessment—and especially in the rigorous evaluative inquiry of DCM—has the potential to teach teachers more powerfully than any conference, course, book, or other method of professional development. Coming face to face with colleagues, reading and debating with them your judgments of students' writing, putting your rhetorical values on the line and advocating for them, and listening to others do the same—these intense collegial activities lead to professional growth for teachers of writing unlike any other experience. Instructors become more aware of their own evaluative landscapes; they learn how others often evaluate and interpret texts very differently; and they work together to forge pedagogical policy on such sticky issues as revision policies, how to value in-class timed writing in a portfolio, and plagiarism. Participants in a recent DCM process wrote of their experiences: "Helpful to hammer things out with colleagues" and "This was the kind of conversation the RC [rhetoric and composition] faculty needed to be doing all along. Certainly we don't need to be grading in lock-step, but we do need to talk about what we value and what we ask of students." DCM also leads to a sense of ownership and belonging on the part of writing instructors—including teaching assistants and adjuncts—who see that they have a strong voice and a crucial role in articulating their program's values. Plus, DCM is fun—an intellectual, rhetorical, and pedagogical party: "Enjoyed listening to my colleagues and working through this together," wrote another recent participant.

3. *Program Development and Evaluation.* DCM provides unprecedented quantity and quality of information about what goes on in a writing program—and how that program could be usefully changed. We learn about how instructors teach, how they evaluate students' work, and how they

believe teaching and evaluation should evolve. City University learned that several values highlighted in the mission statement of the First-Year English Program—Revision, Significance, Mechanics, and Sentences— were indeed taught and valued. On the other hand, DCM at City University also revealed serious disagreements among faculty regarding how and when to value *Revision* (we also learned *why* they disagreed) and highlighted that *Mechanics* received disproportionate quantitative and qualitative emphasis. And nearly the entire issue of Contextual Criteria discussed in chapter 4 was new knowledge. Thus DCM is an unusually rich resource for guiding the growth of any writing program. In stark contrast to the powerfully conserving and stabilizing effect of traditional five-point rubrics, DCM also promotes growth and transformation of writing programs by asking faculty and administrators periodically to revisit and revise their maps, discovering new criteria, eliminating or merging others, and detecting hitherto unknown interrelationships among those criteria.

4. More Valid Assessment of Students' Writing. Over the past decade, many schools, colleges, and universities have moved toward portfolio assessment and communal assessment of students' writing. These developments mark significant and dramatic shifts in the theory and practice of evaluation in our field, especially developments in theories of validity (see Moss 1992). DCM builds on portfolio and communal assessment and improves it by moving us beyond rubrics, traditionally the main obstacle to telling the full and true story of how writing is valued. DCM continues progress in composition toward more valid assessment that coordinates teaching and evaluation to better serve the needs of students, faculty, and the public. By drawing a programmatic representation of values directly from instructors' accounts of how they teach and assess writing in their classrooms, DCM strengthens the bonds between how writing is taught and assessed. It supports best practices (such as revision, response, choice, and writing to real audiences) in the teaching of writing by institutionalizing those values on the program's criteria map. By delving deeper and providing a fuller and truer account of rhetorical and pedagogical values, DCM also strengthens the link between what we tell students and the public about teaching and assessing writing and what we really do. On all these points, we gain truthfulness and therefore validity.

5. Relations with the Public. Because the public (parents, legislators, media, businesses, unions, and everyone else) pays for education, the public wants and deserves to know what goes on in writing programs (among other educational efforts). Why should the public be satisfied with a traditional rubric or scoring guide as an answer to its legitimate questions about composition instruction? DCM provides a relatively compact, accessible portrait of the true complexity and power of rhetorical instruction and evaluation. Though it has the potential to reveal some of our vulnerabilities and secrets (that we don't always agree and that we evaluate students according to Contextual as well as Textual criteria), DCM will ultimately gain us stronger trust and support from the public by showing them the truth, as well as the power and complexity, of what we do in writing programs. Maps of what we really value will simultaneously educate the public about important features of our discipline and our teaching practice, thus protecting us from misunderstanding and undervaluation, two problems frequently encountered by writing programs. Put simply, Dynamic Criteria Maps should help convince the public that teaching writing is not confined to eliminating errors and writing formulaic essays. It could reconnect our society with how rhetoric really works in the world—to create knowledge, understanding, and opinion, and thus to guide our actions—and help us leave behind the diminished, truncated understanding widespread among the public.

DCM is a rigorous method of inquiry into rhetorical values, offering us substantial educational, ethical, political advantages over traditional rubrics as well as over rubric-free assessment.

LIMITS AND STRENGTHS OF DYNAMIC CRITERIA MAPPING

Before discussing strategies for Dynamic Criteria Mapping, I wish to offer some reflections and cautions regarding how we should generate and use DCMs. A DCM carries with it an odd mix of power and powerlessness, usefulness and uselessness, depending on who has created the DCM, who plans to use it, and how it is to be used. The DCM presented and discussed in chapters 3 and 4 is true to the details and nuances of discussions and judgments of the numerous texts that came before evaluators at City University. As a result, this map offers insight into the rhetorical values at play in the classrooms and offices of the FYE Program that autumn. If those at City University wished to take up the DCM presented here and refine and develop it, it would yield even more significance and power for teachers and learners in that writing program. (Since the DCM offered here is new, it remains to be seen whether the real "City University" will do so.)

What this DCM cannot do, and must not be used to do, is guide a different writing program staffed by different instructors, teaching different students, and evaluating different texts. The act and process of Dynamic Criteria Mapping is wholly and usefully portable among writing programs; the specific map of City University presented in the preceding pages is not. The map itself as an artifact is tailored with care from a specific set of conversations about a specific set of texts. For this reason alone, to import a DCM from one program to another would be a tremendous theoretical and pedagogical blunder. Even more important, administrators and instructors in every writing program absolutely must undertake this process for themselves. Others' DCMs can be valuable materials for use in one's own mapping process. Without growing your DCM locally, however, you miss out on the major benefits for professional development, community building, quality of instruction, student learning, and public relations promised by Dynamic Criteria Mapping as a process and an activity. As cartographer James R. Carter states (paraphrasing Phillip C. Muehrcke), "when individuals make their own maps they will learn more about maps and mapping than when looking at maps made by others."

For readers persuaded that DCM is worth the manageable additional investment of resources it requires, all that remains is to discuss how they might undertake the process.

HOW TO CONDUCT DYNAMIC CRITERIA MAPPING

> *If any single caveat can alert map users to their unhealthy but widespread naivete, it is that a single map is but one of an indefinitely large number of maps that might be produced for the same situation or from the same data.*
>
> Monmonier, *How to Lie with Maps* (emphasis original)

As my earlier description of research context and methods showed, I undertook a full-fledged qualitative inquiry into the dynamics of City University's rhetorical values. Employing grounded theory methodology, I spent months collecting and sifting data and more months interpreting those data and refining my analyses of them. I do not expect exceedingly busy instructors and administrators in writing programs to replicate my methods. Instead, I propose here a *streamlined* form of qualitative inquiry that will yield results more limited in detail and scope but still extremely informative and useful to administrators, instructors, and students (for starters).

The best news is that writing programs that regularly conduct communal writing assessment also already do the vast majority of the work of DCM. A few moderate changes in philosophy, terminology, and procedure will provide these writing programs with all the pedagogical, ethical, and political benefits of moving beyond rubrics. For purposes of professional development, community building, open evaluative inquiry, axiological reflection, and accurate and detailed reporting to students and the wider public, a handful of principles and methods will suffice.

Return to Where We Began: Princeton, 1961

Poetically, we can return to the 1961 study by Diederich, French, and Carlton to find an outstanding model for most of the methods used in Dynamic Criteria Mapping. Recall that those researchers collected a large number of *diverse* student texts, submitted them to a dramatically *diverse* group of *distinguished* readers, and submitted those readers' comments on *what they liked and didn't like* in the student papers to careful and thorough analysis. In fact, there is considerable overlap between the original "[fifty-five] categories of comments" Diederich, French, and Carlton drew from readers' evaluations and the forty-seven Textual Criteria I found at City University, as documented in chapter 3. Here is a quick sampling of their "raw" (unreduced) criteria:

Relevance
Development
Too brief or too long
Persuasiveness
Ending
Spelling
Organization
Maturity
Mechanics
Sincerity
Grammar
Clichés
(24)

Note that every one of these criteria identified by Diederich, French, and Carlton corresponds with one or more of the Textual Qualities arranged in my Dynamic Criteria Map or on the list of Textual Features. In other words, up to a crucial point, Diederich, French, and Carlton provide an outstanding model for inquiries like those that I advocate.

Having applauded Diederich, French, and Carlton for their methods and findings, I must also point out that not only are City

University's criteria informed by far more data than Diederich, French, and Carlton's but the criteria represented here are more nuanced, complex, and robust than those presented in the 1961 report and better grounded in the raw data. Note, for example, that I provide lists of verbatim excerpts (synonyms and antonyms) that made up each criterion. I also believe that my organization of instructors' comments into criteria and my arrangement of criteria into constellation simply makes more sense than Diederich's scheme. For example, the Diederich criterion "Too brief or too long," which obviously corresponds with my criterion *Length/Amount (of Text)*, is grouped in the ETS report under "IDEAS." I would expect quantity of text instead to be part of the category "FORM." "Punctuation" and "Grammar" Diederich places under "MECHANICS," which makes good sense to me. But why would another mechanical concern, "Spelling" be listed under "FLAVOR"? Unsurprisingly, the ETS report was also completely bare of Contextual Criteria. Why would positivist psychometricians look at context? To do so would be to make an inexplicable and inappropriate paradigmatic leap. By contrast, DCM is strong on context.

Where contemporary investigators must firmly part ways with Diederich, French, and Carlton is in the ETS team's rapid turn toward scores and statistical methods in an effort to "reduce the complexities" (15) they encountered and to prevent such complexities from corrupting future assessment efforts. Contemporary writing programs need to discover, document, and negotiate their evaluative landscape before they move to standardize and simplify it—if indeed they choose to do the latter at all. Dynamic Criteria Mapping provides the theory and methods for this new sort of effort.

Other Background for DCM

The model for Dynamic Criteria Mapping presented in the following pages builds directly upon a range of sources, which I wish to acknowledge directly and appreciatively. First, DCM assumes that first-year composition courses include a substantial component of communal writing assessment, including reading sample texts, debating the judgment of sample texts in large groups, and negotiating evaluations of live texts in small groups (see the "Research Context" section of chapter 2). This was the example set by administrators and instructors at City University, which in turn was closely and explicitly modeled on Belanoff and Elbow's (Belanoff and Elbow 1991, Elbow and Belanoff, 1991) descriptions of their portfolio assessment program. For a host of reasons, I view these programs of teaching and assessing first-year composition as a models in their own right. Since neither City University's nor SUNY Stonybrook's inquiries into their own values produced a detailed and nuanced axiological record, however, Dynamic Criteria Mapping changes and adds several key theoretical and practical elements to the process.

The opening chapter of this book identifies many theorists of evaluation who have influenced my work and who made possible the ways of thinking about assessment that led to the DCM approach. But DCM also builds on and extends several specific *methods* of evaluative inquiry available in the literature. I have already addressed how *Factors in Judgments of Writing Ability* contributes to and corresponds with DCM methods and how DCM departs from and transcends Diederich's techniques. Guba and Lincoln's *Fourth Generation Evaluation* also powerfully informs the model I present here. Guba and Lincoln provide extensive theoretical grounding for such a "constructivist inquiry," and their method of directing various interest groups to construct their own views of whatever is being assessed helps to guide my vision of how DCM can work. DCM makes a distinctive contribution to and extends beyond Fourth Generation Evaluation in requiring various groups and individuals to work together to synthesize their diverse evaluative perspectives into a single, authoritative document: the map. This difference is most important for students, who would have difficulty using and learning from a complex, unresolved collection of documents like Guba and Lincoln's.

Likewise, in the realm of classroom-based DCM, I find inspiration in Walvoord and Anderson's *Effective Grading*. Although, as I explain later, I see the need to go further than Walvoord and Anderson toward genuine evaluative inquiry in the classroom—especially in how students' knowledge is solicited—many of their methods correspond to, support, and inform the DCM approach.

Below I describe in some detail the specific strategies and options I recommend for administrators and faculty who wish to pursue DCM and thereby tell a fuller story about writing assessment in their writing programs. These methods diverge from traditional methods for large-scale writing assessment (see White) because the goals and the theories that inform them are different. Whereas traditional rubric development seems to focus on qualities of students' texts, Dynamic Criteria Mapping brings to light the dynamics by which instructors assess students' writing. DCM therefore constitutes a "phenomenology of shared writing assessment" (Elbow 2001).

Selecting Sample Texts

Whether your writing program focuses on single essays or collected portfolios, you probably already collect sample texts for instructors to read and discuss in "calibration" or "norming" sessions. Along with rubrics or scoring guides, sample texts are, after all, a standard feature of psychometric writing assessment and are therefore nearly universal to shared evaluation. The key difference in selecting sample texts for hermeneutic assessment and for Dynamic Criteria Mapping is what qualities and features you are looking for in the sample texts.

Traditions of writing assessment dictate that sample texts serve several closely related purposes: sample texts should feature the rhetorical elements highlighted in the rubric; they should demonstrate the full range of writing ability instructors are likely to encounter later in "live" grading; and they should lead instructors to clarity, agreeability, and speed in their judgments.

As explained in chapter 1 (and in Broad 2000), these are not the goals of hermeneutic writing assessment, nor do they fit well with the goals of DCM. For the purpose of DCM is to discover, negotiate, and publish the truth about the evaluative topography of any given writing program, not to turn away from complexity and dissent in judgments. Therefore, those who select sample texts for discussion need to look for very different features from those found on the traditional menu.

Sample texts for DCM should be selected because they feature as many *kinds* of rhetorical successes and failures as possible. If those selecting sample texts are aware of criteria that are particularly important to their writing program (for example, significance, voice, detail, growth, mechanics), they should look for sample texts that exhibit (or fail to exhibit) those qualities. Finally, and perhaps most important (and most unlike psychometric assessment), the group selecting sample texts should not shun texts about which readers are likely to disagree in their judgments. On the contrary, these are crucial papers to include in the large-group discussions that precede live grading. For only by openly discussing, debating, and negotiating evaluative differences can a writing program move genuinely and with integrity toward increased evaluative coherence and community.

All these considerations in selecting sample texts point to the need for the group of faculty and others in charge of selecting texts to be as diverse as possible in institutional status: professors, adjuncts, TAs, undergraduate students. The group should also represent the full range of rhetorical interests evident in the writing program: correctivists, expressivists, creative writers, technical writers, literature instructors. Because of their power position in the writing program, administrators should probably play a limited role or be altogether absent from the process of selecting sample texts for discussion in Dynamic Criteria Mapping. Finally, the group for selecting sample texts should change with each round of DCM, so as to get as much diversity as possible in the texts and their qualities.

Articulation in Large Groups

In "Pulling Your Hair Out: Crises of Standardization in Communal Writing Assessment" (Broad 2000), I proposed changing the name of large-group discussions that precede live grading from "standardization," "calibration," or "norming" to *"articulation."* The traditional names for these discussions point toward only part of their appropriate function: exploring how evaluators *agree.* These names neglect an equally important part of those discussions that has heretofore remained hidden and forbidden: exploring how and why evaluators disagree. In the current context, with its emphasis on making assessment fit with and support classroom teaching, communal writing assessment must explore both these aspects of shared evaluation. The word "articulation" refers to both how things are joined and how they are separated. That word also refers to the process by which writing instructors discover and come to voice what they value in their students' work.

Once sample texts have been selected, copied, and distributed, and once instructors and administrators have read the sample texts and made notes on what they value and do not value in each text, they are ready to meet for articulation. In articulation sessions, participants discuss the specific criteria by which they were guided in reaching their pass/fail decisions about each text. While they should note and discuss evaluative agreement and disagreement, they do not need to ensure that everyone agrees on how a particular text should be judged. Instead, each participant should focus on *listening to* and *understanding* the full range of values at work in the program, and each participant should actively *reflect* on how the values discussed might inform her future teaching and assessment of writing. Articulation constitutes no more or less than a powerfully transformative professional conversation.

Trios for Live Judgments

Before examining in more detail how discussions of sample texts lead to a Dynamic Criteria Map, we need to consider how trio meetings conducting "live grading" should figure in. Most of the work of collecting and analyzing data will take place in the large-group articulation sessions. Since trios are responsible for live grading of students with which each trio-mate has worked in the classroom, instructors have more, and more pressing, responsibilities when meeting in trios than they do when participating in articulation sessions.

We must therefore expect trios to contribute somewhat less to the DCM process than do articulation sessions. Trios should still maintain keen awareness of the criteria that arise in their discussions of texts. All trio-mates should keep notes on those criteria they mention or hear, and trio-mates can check in with each other at the conclusion of their meetings to compare and compile notes. Trios should then report their data to program administrators or DCM leaders, who can help instructors integrate trio findings into the DCM process. In this fashion, trios play an important role in DCM by confirming, refuting, or complicating the preliminary map generated in articulation sessions. The articulation and trio meetings are therefore mutually informative and transformative.

Collecting Data for Dynamic Criteria Mapping

As I described in chapter 2, my method for studying City University included tape recordings and transcriptions of norming sessions, trio meetings, and solo interviews. Such data gathering requires a large investment of time and energy, which I assume is unavailable to most writing programs. I therefore recommend the following streamlined techniques for gathering data on what we really value in students' writing.

From among all the instructors who have prepared for articulation by reading and judging sample texts, two should volunteer to act as scribes. These scribes should stand where the large articulation group can clearly see them. Using whatever technology is available (marker boards, chalkboards, flip charts, or computers projected onto a screen), scribes should write down the specific criteria to which readers refer when they explain why they passed or failed a particular sample text. Scribes should also note the specific passage in the specific sample text to which a participant refers when invoking one or more criteria. These references to sample texts will become important features of the final publication that emerges from DCM. Non-scribes should attend to scribes' work and provide correction and elaboration where necessary, so that the scribes' records reflect instructors' criteria as fully and accurately as possible.

Scribes must carefully avoid synthesizing, organizing, or conceptualizing how various criteria are interrelated. That work comes later, during data analysis. Their job during data collection is to identify and record the full range of rhetorical criteria (textual, contextual, and other) informing judgments of students' writing. Scribes' work should be carefully saved and made available to all participants at, or shortly after, the conclusion of the articulation session. If data analysis (see below) does not take place immediately following articulation, instructors should be able to carry these raw data into trio meetings and work from them and add to them during trios.

Analyzing Data for Dynamic Criteria Mapping

As with the data gathering methods described in the preceding section, I believe that a relatively simple and quick version of data analysis will provide instructors and administrators with high-quality knowledge and insight regarding how composition is taught and evaluated in their writing programs.

Ideally, data analysis for DCM would take place after all the teaching and evaluation for a particular course were complete. Instructors would be fresh from the intense experience of finishing a course—and particularly of evaluating students' portfolios—and would therefore be more keenly attuned than at any other time to their rhetorical and pedagogical values. Perhaps between terms, then, instructors would come together to view the raw data collected during articulation sessions and trio sessions. If between terms proves to be an unworkable time for instructors to meet, instructors could make notes on the documented raw data regarding additions, corrections, and connections they can offer based on their experiences at the end of the term.

Preferably in small groups, participants would then try to establish the identities, contents, boundaries, and interrelationships of the various criteria on which their evaluative decisions were made. They might discover large categories of criteria like or unlike mine (Textual, Contextual, Other). They might find more, fewer, or different rhetorical criteria. They might perceive different relationships among criteria and therefore create different constellations. And their constellations might, in turn, be differently interrelated. Some criteria might be mapped two- or three-dimensionally, and others might be adequately represented by simple lists.

Analyzing data is the most intense work of Dynamic Criteria Mapping. Everything depends on being true to the data collected, yet analysis also invites participants to perceive, interpret, judge, and compose meaningful findings out of those data. Data analysis is a highly critical and creative activity that carries with it unparalleled power to understand and guide the writing program and the teaching and learning going on within it. And most important, it provides administrators, instructors, and students with an unprecedented opportunity to know how evaluation really works in their program. By the end of the process, participants are usually tired but also excited about and gratified by the valuable new knowledge they have produced.

A caution: in my experiences helping faculty map their values, data analysis is where most, if not all, of the preceding work can be lost or wasted. The danger is that participants will be tempted to import familiar, comfortable, and simplified schemes by which to arrange the criteria they generated during articulation. In their chapter "Analyzing Interpretive Practice," Gubrium and Hostein quote Schutz on the crucial importance of protecting participants' experiences from being interpreted in hasty or imported ways.

> Schutz argues that the social sciences should focus on the ways that the life world—the world every individual takes for granted—is experienced by its members. He cautions that "the safeguarding of [this] subjective point of view is the only but sufficient guarantee that the world of social reality will not be replaced by a fictional non-existing world constructed by the scientific observer" (8).

Repeatedly, I have witnessed DCM participants rushing to fit the "social reality" (raw data) of what instructors have said they valued with a "fictional non-existent world" of what they thought about what they valued before DCM even began. Yet the whole DCM project aims to move us beyond what we think about how we value students' writing and to discover what and how we really value.

The best technique for "safeguarding" the integrity of the raw data is for the analysts to work slowly and methodically from those data through small steps of abstraction and conceptualization. For example, they would want to ponder carefully whether comments that texts are "interesting," "lively," "surprising," and "creative" really belong together as a single criterion-cluster (as I concluded they did). At each step of conceptualization, they should check their category against the data they wish to gather there. Once participants have generated a collection of criterion-clusters, they can then work at discerning interrelationships among them, again with the same cautions against importing conceptual schemes and the same urgent plea that mappers induce their concepts with tenderness and care from the raw data before them.

Debating and Negotiating Evaluative Differences

Once participant-researchers have collected and analyzed their data, creating their categories, lists, and maps of rhetorical criteria, they need to undertake one more step before finalizing and publishing their results. Now that they know, perhaps for the first time, how they *do* value students' writing, they need to undertake high-powered professional discussions regarding how they *should* value that writing. In other words, their focus shifts at this point from the descriptive to the normative. This is the stage at which their professional insight and wisdom may have the greatest impact.

In presenting my DCM findings from City University, I highlighted those dynamics that I believed required debate and, if possible, a decision one way or another on the part of the program. A few examples include:

To what extent should whether a student fulfilled the assignment count for or against her?

Which should influence judgments more: in-class, unrevised, unedited texts or texts whose writing processes included drafting, response, research, revision, and proofreading?

How should perceptions of learning, progress, and growth figure into judgments of students' rhetorical performances?

What should be the weight and role of mechanics in the program's teaching and assessment of students' writing abilities?

These are the sorts of questions that deserve and require the professional attention of administrators and instructors in a program *before* they publicize their findings.

As with all aspects of teaching and assessing writing, consensus on these issues will be difficult to achieve. Minority reports and dissenting opinions may therefore be useful elements of the DCM that emerges from these discussions. The main point is for instructors to be on the alert for criteria around which various dynamics, especially differences among instructors, put students at risk of being unfairly penalized. Since student learning is the heart of what we do, it needs to be the reference point for discussions by which writing programs not only record and discover but also shape and refine what they value in students' writing.

Publicizing, Learning, and Teaching from the Dynamic Criteria Map

Following its debate and negotiation of the DCM, a writing program will be ready to publish its map along with the sample texts that informed it. It should be made as simple and accessible as possible, especially to students, while still maintaining enough texture, nuance, detail, and complexity to be true to the evaluative dynamics it claims to represent. The Dynamic Criteria Map document that emerges is likely to include:

1. An introduction or preface written by one or more instructors or administrators explaining the goals, methods, and virtues of Dynamic Criteria Mapping
2. The constellations and lists of specific rhetorical criteria, including lists of synonyms and antonyms where available and references to sample texts to illustrate what each criterion looks like "in action"
3. Full sample texts discussed in articulation sessions (and perhaps one or two additional texts submitted by instructors from their trio sessions)
4. Other program documents (mission statements, syllabi, publications) useful to students and others who wish to understand what is taught and valued in the writing program

When a writing program's DCM is widely published and shared among students, writing faculty, other faculty, and the public, it should provide fodder for energetic dialogue regarding teaching and assessing composition. The DCM can informatively drive program assessment and design, as well as the rhetorical development of individual students. Here lies another avenue for future research: tracing the uses and perceptions of the DCM process and the DCM document by faculty, students, and others.

Revising the DCM

To be truly *dynamic*, a DCM needs to grow and change organically over time. Therefore, writing programs should treat their maps as works in progress and should adjust and enhance them periodically. Some programs might conduct full-scale DCM every year, with multiple sample texts and large groups of instructors; others might read just one or two new sample texts each year or convene smaller instructor groups; others still might go longer between mapping sessions. The point is to keep the process going so that the DCM reflects the program's rhetorical values steadily more faithfully and so that the DCM keeps up with inevitable—and desirable—changes in the program's framework of values.

CLASSROOM DCM

Whether or not a writing program conducts communal writing assessment, instructors in that program can still conduct Dynamic Criteria Mapping. When shared evaluation is not an option, classroom-based DCM may be the only method for documenting and reflecting on an instructor's evaluative framework. Walvoord and Anderson present superb strategies for making assessment educational and supportive of key learning goals. Much of their language and thinking could serve as a guide for the work described in this book.

> We urge faculty to abandon false hopes that grading can be easy, uncomplicated, uncontested, or one-dimensional. Teachers must manage the power and complexity of the grading system rather than ignore or deny it. (xvii)

and

> [W]e place grading within the frame of *classroom research*—a term used for a teacher's systematic attempt to investigate the relationship between teaching and learning in her or his classroom. (xvii; emphasis original)

Walvoord and Anderson offer powerful conceptions of how instructors can make assessment into research, which in turn informs teaching and learning. I find their method for managing the power and complexity of assessment limited, however, by the nature of the "systematic investigation," or inquiry, the authors suggest.

Note, for example, that instructors are urged to "identify" (67), "choose," and "ask themselves" (68) about the evaluative criteria for primary trait analysis, which will guide students in fulfilling assignments and guide the instructor in evaluating students' work. A basic principle out of which I developed Dynamic Criteria Mapping is that people do not have satisfactory access to their rhetorical values by sitting and reflecting on them. Instead, people need to enter into discussion and debate of actual performances in an effort to discover what they (and others) value.

To their credit, Walvoord and Anderson recommend that instructors include colleagues (70) and students in the construction of evaluation schemes. "We know faculty who like to involve their students in establishing criteria for student work" (86). Unfortunately, the mildly condescending tone of the phrase "like to involve their students" is reflected in the methods proposed. Students are asked about what they believe good performance looks like in general, rather than what they know about the instructor's evaluative framework.

This last point is the key to classroom DCM. Near the end of a course, instructors should ask their students to gather data (handouts, responses to writing, comments made in class) that answer the question: "What does this instructor (who wields the institutional power of the course grade) value in your work?" Students in this model are taken as more authoritative sources for answering this question than the instructor because students hold more data on what the instructor *really* values as opposed to what the instructor *thinks* she values. Beyond this key difference in data gathering, the process for classroom DCM closely parallels the process described above for programmatic DCM.

EPILOGUE

Our society's orientation toward educational evaluation is undergoing a paradigm shift, away from the technical requirements and justifications of positivist psychometrics and toward considerations such as how well assessments support best practices in teaching and learning. In this context, we owe it to ourselves, our students, our colleagues, and our supporters in the wider society to take advantage of these shifts and to develop new methods of writing assessment to illustrate *"that knowledge is complex, ambiguous, and socially constructed in a context"* (Baxter Magolda, 195; Baxter Magolda's emphasis). Dynamic Criteria Mapping is one of those new methods. It will help us move into a new era of writing assessment in which the endeavors of teaching and assessing writing are theoretically and ethically aligned and are therefore mutually supportive.

In the end, Dynamic Criteria Mapping does for writing assessment what the technology of writing did several thousand years ago for human thought and language: captures it, sets it down on paper, makes it into a concrete object that can be reflected on, interpreted, shared, discussed, negotiated, and revised. As a profession, we are ready for this new technique because we have developed theoretical approaches that allow us to embrace complexity and make it meaningful. We no longer need to turn away, panic-stricken, from the rich and context-bound truth of how experts really assess writing. Instead, we can face that truth equipped with tools (qualitative inquiry) and attitudes (hermeneutics) that help us tap the energy of apparent chaos without being consumed by it. We can embrace the life of things:

> You are fabulous creatures, each and every one.
> And I bless you: *More Life.*
> The Great Work Begins.
>
> END OF PLAY
> 			(Kushner 146, emphasis original)

NOTES

1. Some of the text, figures, and tables in this chapter originally appeared in Broad, 2000. These excerpts, copyright 2000 by the National Council of Teachers of English, are reprinted with permission.

2. Sample texts selected for inclusion here are those that received the most attention in the norming and trio conversations I analyzed.

3. Synonyms and antonyms for each criterion are direct quotations from transcripts; words added for clarity are bracketed. Where synonyms and antonyms contain no internal punctuation, I have separated them with commas. Where they do contain internal punctuation, I have separated them with semicolons.

4. *Learning/Progress/Growth* is a Contextual Criterion discussed further in chapter 4.

5. In this study I define "criteria for evaluation" as "considerations influencing judgments of writing performance."

6. "Video Notes" were taken from videotapes of norming sessions and added as supplementary data to the audio transcripts.

Appendix A
ASSIGNMENTS FOR ENGLISH 1 ESSAYS

ASSIGNMENT 1: A SIGNIFICANT EVENT

Subject: In this essay you will recount some event from your past
            that has particular significance for you. Generally, such
            pieces fall under the category of "How I got to be the way
            I am . . ." or "The day I learned a lesson . . ." or "Why I
            changed my mind . . ."; that is, they are examples of expe-
            riences that have shaped your identity or your values.

            You will use narrative and description, but your purpose
            will be reflective. You may choose to explicitly name the
            change or realization you experienced, or you may leave it
            implicit in the essay.

Audience: Think of writing this for submission to an anthology of
            outstanding essays by college students.

Length: Roughly 750 words.

Due: Draft for discussion

            Paper to be evaluated

ASSIGNMENT 2: A PORTRAIT

Subject: In this assignment you will present a portrait of a person
            who is, for some reason, important in your life. You will
            describe, but you will also narrate, because events and
            actions define people as much as physical description. You
            will probably want to put your character in action and to
            show us people's responses to this character. You may
            want us to hear the sound of your character's voice.

            Think again about focusing and "telling facts," the details
            that make us see and *hear* and *feel*.

Audience: Again, think of writing an essay that might be selected for
                our text, one written for an audience of literate college
                students as a model of expository prose.

Length: Roughly 750 words.

Due: Draft

                Final form

ASSIGNMENT 3: PROBLEM/SOLUTION

Subject: Write an essay proposing a solution to a particular prob-
                lem. Look for something close at hand, a problem that
                really does affect you. For this paper your audience will
                have to be quite specific, a person or group who might be
                in a position to help solve the problem.

Length: 750 words

Due: Draft

                Final

ASSIGNMENT 4: EVALUATION

Subject: For this assignment you will be asked to write an evalua-
                tion *in class*. You may bring with you a text and/or notes
                on the subject of your evaluation.

                Think of this essay as a piece of writing for an audience
                who reads *The Evening Herald*. This may be a review of a
                cultural event, an evaluation of some feature of life on
                campus, a course, a teacher, a text, a fast-food chain, or a
                french fry.

                Again, in this essay you wish to persuade, to present your
                judgment with authority, detail, clarity and conviction.

Due: In class

ASSIGNMENT 5: A PROFILE

Subject: This last paper for the course is to be a profile; that is, it
                will be a description of a specific person, place, or activity.
                Generally, profiles urge us to see something new in a sub-
                ject; they often involve surprise or contrast, a perspective

on the subject that forces us to re-evaluate it. They are close-ups with a very strong controlling theme.

Choose something accessible; use field notes and/or interviews; spend time shaping your material to arouse reader interest and curiosity. ("The best beginnings are surprising and specific.")

Length: 3 – 5 pages

Due: Draft
Final

Anguish

I go to bed that night, July 22 at about 11:00. All night I toss and turn. For some reason I can't get to sleep. It's 12:00, 1:00, then 2:00. Finally at about 5:00 in the morning I feel like I'm getting in a deep sleep.

Ring! Ring!

"Hello" I answered drowsily.

"Meeky?" the voice said.

"What do you want Diane (my aunt) my mother is not over here" I said.

"Meeky?" asked Diane.

"What's wrong?" I asked worriedly.

"Karen just called NaNa and she said that David had been shot and killed."

I drop the phone screaming and crying, " No," All I could do was ask why? Why him? My husband woke up and asked me what was wrong. My eyes were so filled with tears that I couldn't even see his face. My sister came in and asked the same question. I told her. We put some clothes on and out of the house by 7:00 a.m., to go over to University Hospital to view the body.

I left the building hoping and praying that they notified the wrong David Malcolm's mother. I began thinking about my uncle's situation. When he was young he was quite stupid. He had two girlfriends who were both pregnant. My uncle chose to marry Karen. But Cathy had her baby first and she named her baby David. Karen, a couple of months later, had her baby and she named her baby David, also. But the catch was he was the III. And a Malcolm, I might add. Cathy's last name was Phillips. Since she hadn't married my uncle, therefore her baby's full name was David

Phillips. Everybody grew up knowing this (But things happen and people changed and my uncle and Karen got divorced. Several years later he married Cathy. Cathy changed her son's name to be like his father David Malcolm except with out the Jr.) I hoped for the best

But all my hopes were let down and too late. But because it was my cousin David lying on that cold table with that sheet pulled up to his neck. He was the one I shared all my childhood memories with. He was the one who I grew up with inside of our family circle. I told my husband that who ever did it had the wrong David. By this time all of my immediate family were there except my uncle and his wife and their David. I left the morgue feeling nauseated.

I couldn't get in because my sister had the keys to my apartment. Because I didn't want to upset my brother in law's children, I went over to my grandmother's house. My mother comes to get me and I leave. With in all this time it's only 10:30 a.m. and I felt old. I had a hair appointment so I decided to go. My cousin Kim picks me up. We go back to my house and sit. Everybody has seen the 12:00 news and each station gave information that was wrong. So Kim and my sister Toshia called up the different stations and corrected the information. Five o'clock rolls around and we're watching channel 12 "Two fatal shootings." 'Sshh, sshh'! "David Anderson Malcolm III was shot and killed early this morning on Fox Creek and Blue Hill Rd. Silence falls upon us there's nothing said.

It was the beginning of the week. I was expecting to see my cousin that Friday and Saturday night downtown at the Jazz Festival. My week / life was crushed. I treated the rest of the week as if I were going to a wedding. Which is exactly what I felt like, and even thought on that Friday the day of his wake.

I got to the parlor and walk in I see his body in the casket, but it still didn't click in my head that he was gone. I see a picture of him and start to hyperventilate and scream and cry.

At about 6:00 the family lines up to go in. My aunt who was six months pregnant is in line in front of me; she fainted. I saw his face with make-up and that stretched smile on his face. I jumped and jumped until I couldn't jump any more. I tried to jump the pain out of my heart but I guess that tactic failed because he's still gone. The funeral procession begins and ends all to soon. They started to close the casket. I knew that he wasn't breathing and never would be any more. But I had the feeling that he was going to suffocate in that small space. I prayed they wouldn't close it. (Closing the casket and the burial was the hardest things for me to deal with. Because it made it so final.)

Saturday morning at about 7:30 in the morning we get up to get dress for the burial. By 9:30 we're all there ready to go to the cemetery. I see the hearse and go to pieces because in that car is my cousin. We take a drive to a cemetery in Mt Prospect.

To see where they were going to put him broke my heart even more. I was so expecting to seeing him on my birthday. But not this way, not in a casket or in a cemetery.

Gramma Sally

Have you every known someone who is like a matriarch of the family. They are held in esteemed honor and everyone loves them. My great-grandmother Gramma Sally is this person. Her name is Sally Laurel, but my family calls her Gramma. My whole family has a great respect for her. They love her dearly. I love her because she is my grandmother, but I don't really know her. She immigrated to the United States from Poland, during World War II, with her family. From the stories I heard about her; I built in my mind this picture of this great woman who had won battles and saved lives with her many contributions. If she had accomplished these feats; I was sorely disappointed when I saw her. Gramma is a short, frumpy woman that wears cat-eye glasses. Her flowery dresses and moppy, grey hair look like a bad Halloween costume. Her personality is also in need of improvement for the great woman she is. She is a very bitter and sarcastic person that is always yelling for no reason. She supposedly loves children. I find that hard to believe since she is always shooing us away. "Go away children I'm talking, can't you go outside and make all that noise. Your giving me a headache." she would yell at my cousins and I. My mother always told me as I got older I would understand and appreciate her. I didn't believe her and my dislike for my grandmother began.

When I was thirteen years old Gramma came to stay with us during my cousins Bar Mitzvah. I hadn't seen her in over five years. My chance was here to finally get to know her. I was going to give us a chance to get along. I was very wrong. From the moment she walked through the door the complaining began. Nothing in our house was good enough for her. She wanted to cook for herself. She said my mom's food was to spicy. My parents worked so I stayed home to make sure Gramma would be okay. I stayed in my room a lot; coming out once in a while to check on Gramma and get her some lunch. We would sit and watch soaps while she ate. We watched the same soaps so we would discuss our favorite characters. One day I was in my room listening to my records; and I heard my dog barking. I thought someone was at the door. I went downstairs to look. I saw my dog, Spike, barking at Gramma. I was about to yell at him, when I noticed her teasing him with lunchmeat from her sandwich. He would try to take it from her hands; and when he got close enough to get it she would kick him as hard as she could. I couldn't believe my eyes. I waited a moment and she did it again. She was laughing like a crazy person. I ran down the stairs screaming. She was surprised to see me. She didn't know what to say. She looked ashamed for a minute; but it went away quickly enough. I couldn't even look at her. I ran upstairs and threw myself on the bed and started crying. I hate her, I really do. She was a mean, hateful woman. To make matters worse my grandma called and said Gramma (her mother) just called her and told her I had been ignoring her while she was calling my name; and that I had forgot to bring her lunch. Then she had the nerve to ask me to put Spike away because he was biting Gramma. I knew she was lieing so I didn't say anything. I was going to wait till my mom got home to handle it.

My mom got home and she saw Gramma first. Gramma told her the cock and bull story also. She came upstairs to talk to me. I told her what really happened. She was very upset by this, but she didn't know what to do. She told me to forget about it. Gramma was a bitter old woman who couldn't come to terms with her weaknesses. I was mad because they didn't say anything to her or yell at her. I was really mad at my parents and I gave them the silent treatment for days. She finally left and I felt as if a great weight had been lifted from me.

I tried to forget about her and what happened. She still sent money on my birthday and on graduation. Then I got an invitation to attend my uncles fund-raiser dinner for his running for state senator of Southern Arizona. I was very excited and left the next week. I was having a lot of fun when my aunt approached one evening and asked if I would do her a big favor. "Will you look after Gramma Sally during the dinner she's not as strong as she used to be." I was shocked by that. I hadn't seen Gramma in four years. She had to be around 90 yrs. old. I knew my aunt didn't know what happened and I would feel bad if I said no. I told her I would do it and regretted it the instant I said it.

The party was beautiful and I was very proud of my uncle. I thought this' won't be so bad. Then I saw Gramma. She looked so old I didn't even

realize who she was at first. The change that had come over her was dras-
tic. I couldn't even hate her when I saw her like this. I just felt remorse
and guilty for hating her all these years and not keeping in tune to how
she was getting along I walked over to her and hugged her after my aunt
did. "You look so beautiful. Just like your mother." she said. She had tears
in her eyes and I didn't know how to react. All the pent up anger I felt
inside just wouldn't completely go away. I pushed her to the dinner table
and we ate. I sat there and listened to her talk to her neighbors at the
table. She was a very intelligent person who knew a wide variety of subjects. I never realized this before. I also never talked to her before. After
dinner We sat next to each other and she grabbed my hand. I was scared
but I didn't want to pull my hand away and hurt her feelings. I felt her
slipping something on my fingers. I looked down and saw her putting her
engagement ring on my finger. It was beautiful. I didn't know what to say.
"This is for you. My favorite granddaughter so you will think of me
always.", she said in a husky voice full of tears. You remind me so much of
myself and the vitality that is no longer in me. When I see you my youth is
brought back to me and everything that I once had is gone. I didn't know
what to say. This woman I hated so much was telling me how much she
loved me. As I sat there I realized she didn't hate me or wanted to be
mean she was just jealous of the life I had ahead of me and upset over the
life that was behind her. I reminded her of herself so much she din't know
whether to love me or hate me for the memories that I dredged up in her.

I don't hate Gramma anymore. I do feel sorry for her. Her vital and
active mind in a body to old to do her any good. Gramma is still alive.
She's 94 yrs. old. I haven't seen her since then, but she still writes and
calls once in a while, so I'll remember she's still around. Her greatest
fear I think is to be forgotten. I'll never forget her. She taught me a lot
about old people and to never judge people to harshly. They might have
a lot of problems which we couldn't begin to perceive.

Pops

As we walked the trail of our 210 acre farm, I looked at my Pops. I saw
a tall man who was slightly stooping because his shoulders had started
to roll forward. He had a ruddy complexion from years of exposure
to the elements. When he smiled, he smiled from ear to ear with a
kind of goofy grin. His eyes always twinkled, as if he had just played
the best practical joke on someone, but at the same time, if one

looked close enough, one could see the wisdom he had gathered through the years.

He and I were having one of our usual long talks about the world and it's woes in general such as how his business was doing and how crazy Saddam Hussein is. My thoughts flashed back to the many walks that we had taken and the many talks that we've shared about everything from how life was when he was a boy to what a great invention ice cream was. Scenes of me as a small child, holding on to his hand and skipping along a gravel road in the summer, with flowers all around, or of me curled up watching TV on his lap at night, or in more recent years, of me asking him what he thought of my newest dream of being a fashion and/or costume designer flashed through my head

Eventually the topic came around to my leaving for school as it had many times in the last few weeks. All of my male friends and relatives were terribly concerned about me coming to the big city by myself, but none were as worried as my dad.

"I grew up in Hillside. I know how dangerous it is for a girl," he said with a concerned look on his usually happy face. "Sarah, I'm not saying this because I don't think you're big enough to take care of yourself, I'm saying it because I love you and I don't want anything to happen to you."

"I know Pops, I'll be fine. Don't worry so much. What should I do that would make you feel better?" I said a patted his hand.

"Well I think you'd be safer if you didn't go out past dark," he said with a mischievous glint in his eyes.

"PAST DARK? Past dark, come on Dad! You don't really think I'm going to stay in past dark, do you?" I protested.

"Well ok, don't stay in past dark, but when you do go out you should have some kind of protection. You aren't allowed to have dogs in the dorm are you?" he asked with a serious look.

"No Pops, no dogs allowed," I sighed in exasperation.

"Ok, then we need to get you a handgun licence so you can carry one with you, concealed," he said with an outright grin on his sunburned face.

"Right Dad, I'll carry around your 357 with the scope, concealed in a shoulder halster on my 5'6" 110lbs. frame. Nobody will see it. Then, when some creep approaches me, I can whip it out and shoot him!" I sarcastically agreed.

This silly argument continued about an hour, and every time I tried to sum up his list of protective "things," it got longer and sillier. In the end he decided that I should have 10 body guards (himself included in this bunch—of course), a dog (a really big and fierce one), and a gun (as loud and as big as I could carry). After another 30 minutes of this discussion, I talked him down to a promise that I wouldn't go out alone after dark.

We have our disagreements like all fathers and daughters do, but Pops has always supported me in all my dreams. He is the one person who will always be honest with me whether he is boosting my ego or criticizing me for some fault in my actions. When I look at myself, I can see part of him.

END TERM PORTFOLIOS

Portfolio 2

When Thinking

When thinking of who to write about, I had some trouble in choosing. To me a person who is significant in my life is someone who has a positive influence on me, can make me laugh, will listen to my problems aay or night, will be totally honest, support my decisions, and knows me better than anyone else. To me, this person is Lela.

People who don't know her as well as I do may think that she is not someone who cares alot about other people or how they feel. Her appearance is very deceiving. She is 5'9", has long curly brown hair, baby blue eyes, a big smile, and is very skinny. Because of the way she dresses people may think she is a snob. Lela always wears the newest style of clothing and her make-up is always perfect.

Over the past two years I have had to make some difficult decisions and been through some trying times, and Lela is the only one I could talk to. An example of how she has always been there for me would be about a year ago when I fell head over heels for her boyfriends best friend. We went out for a while but then he went back to his girlfriend. I was a total wreck for over three months and then Lela stepped in and told me, "Mike isn't worth the tears, one of these days he'll realize what he lost and, he'll come back, just don't put your life on hold for him." Since then, Mike and I have been seeing each other off and on, and Lela has been right there for me and given me a lot of support and been patient with me. Lela has gone through the same type of situations and she never judges me or tells me to forget about him.

Besides the reason I gave, there are many things that make Lela a very important person to me. The one thing I admire most about her is the fact that she can be totally honest with me, but do it in a way that doesn't hurt my feelings. In my situation with Mike, Lela gave me her honest opinion but never tried to change my mind or influence me wrongly. Whenever she tells ie something, I never have to doubt it because I trust her enough to know she would never lie to me. There aren't many people you can say that about these days, but she is one of the few.

Another thing that I like about Lela is her personality and her ability to make me laugh. Whenever I'm upset or feeling really down, she can always cheer me up. She has this sparkling personality and a way of making people feel good about themselves. One way she can make me or anyone else feel better is just by laughing. She has a contagious laugh that will leave your sides aching by the end of a conversation. Lela is always quick with a joke or smart remark that can make an intense discussion turn into a laughing fest.

Lela and I are so close that to say we are like sisters doesn't even come close to it. We are always out together or over each others houses. I'm over her house so much that her dad even once jokingly asked when he had another daughter. Just an example of how close I am to her family, I call her mom, mom and her dad Chip, which is their family nickname for him.

Some people may think that we are a little on the wierd side with things we do, but it's all done in good fun and we never take things too seriously. For example, one night we were coming home from her boyfriends house in Oak Park and we managed to get ourselves lost, something we seem to do frequently. We weren't sure what exit to take, and she took the opposite of what I said, and this is when the adventure started! After we got off the exit, we managed to figure out where we were, we were in the middle of downtown at 2 a.m. on Saturday night. Lela got distracted by something and before we knew it we were going right through a red light. When we realized the light was red, it was too late. To the right of us was a brand new red Stealth coming at us. We managed to escape the fated accident and no one got hurt. While we were shaking with fear, we couldn't help but laugh about it. This just prove my point about us not taking anything to seriously, it was a situation that most normal people would not have laughed at. Anyway, right after this happened we had to pull over because Lela was laughing so hard she couldn't see, and we didn't want to have another near miss. When we finally got home, no one else seemed to think that it was funny!

The reasons I have given for why Lela is a significant person in my life don't do her justice, she is the best friend anyone could ever have.

There are just too many things to say about Lela that I couldn't possibly put them all down on paper. She is my best friend and she knows me better than anyone else does. I know that no matter how far apart we end up we will always be the very best of friends because I can't imagine not having her in my life.

The Clock

The clock in my car read 10:45, I had 15 minutes to get to my first class. What a way to start off the first day of college. When I finally found a place to park I didn't bother to look and see if it was a no parking zone, which it turned out to be. As I looked at my watch it was now 10:50, I began to run as fast as I could. I reached Zimmer Auditorium just as class was beginning, found a place to sit, and tried to catch my breath. When my classes were over for the day, I was able to find one of my friends and she drove me back to my car so I didn't have to walk. When we arrived at the car, I found a parking ticket on my windshield. I just felt like crying, but I didn't.

This is just one example of how hard it is for students to find parking places on the side streets near campus. While not all students have this problem, those of us who do not have a pass, must go through the hassle of finding a place to park every morning.

The main problem with the lots are that the school sells more passes than there are places to park. As I mentioned before this can pose a real problem for students without passes or those who have class later in day. It's a problem because by the time they get to school there are no places left in the lot and they have to park in the garage and may end up being late for class. For exmaple, my friend Christi had to park in the garage one day and was late for her class because the lot she has a pass for was full. To try to solve this problem I propose that the school sell only the same number of passes that there are spots. If this did not go over well, I would also suggest that passes are sold according to the time you have class. I realize that this would face a lot of opposition from the students and faculty because it would be a lot of hassle and they already have enough to deal with If passes were sold by quarters and according to time blocks, it would allow students who have classes in the mid-afternoon to have a place to park. A refutation to this proposal would be that if you pay for a place to park, you shouldn't have to compromise or leave campus as soon as they are finished with their classes. A way to appease people who find a problem with this, would be to reduce the price of the passes.

One final solution to the parking problem would be to have a parking lot for every building. While this would be costly, it would give each student a place to park depending on their major.

One reason the streets are overcrowded is because the students who don't have passes or choose not to park on campus are forced to].eave an hour early to find a place on the streets. I personally have to leave an hour early to park by the hospital and have enough time to walk across campus to get to my classes on time. People who have passes may not think that this is a very big problem, but if they had to go through the routine everyday they would have complaints too.

One other problem that arises from the limited parking spaces is the hassle of dealing with metered parking places. rn the first place, if you are lucky enough to get one, you still have to run out to your car and re-feed the meter before jou get a ticket. The problem with running out to your car is that sometimes you only have 10 minutes between classes and, Once again, you could run the risk of being late for a class.

City University is generally a commuter school, as are most schools. As I said before, I feel that my solutions could work and be beneficial to both students and faculty. The school could also ask for student volunteers to organize a committee to deal with the complaints of commuters. The committee could propose a system of carpools depending on where students live, finding the funds and space to put in more parking lots and to build more garages.

While the solutions I have proposed may face opposition and rejection, I feel, if they are thought over and well presented, they could, as I stated, be very beneficial.

T.G.I. Friday's

This in-class essay was originally hand-written. I (the researcher) re-typed it so I could change place names to protect the anonymity of the writing program under study here. I have faithfully re-created the hand-written essay's punctuation, spelling, and stylistic flourishes.

T.G.I. Friday's is an excellent restaurant on the Brookview side of Big River. Friday's, as it is called, is an enjoyable place for people of all ages.

The atmosphere is one full of fun and night-time excitement. This is my personal favorite restaurant in the area. This place provides an entertaining way to relax and unwind with friends aor family after a long day at work or school. The reason I so highly recommend Friday's is because, as I said, it is a place for people of all ages.

The food is excellent, there is a variety to choose from, prices are reasonable, service is fast and friendly, the view of the river and the city skyline is incredible at night, and the location couldn't be better. Friday's is located near the center of the nightlife on Riverboat Landing. Next to Friday's is a dance club, below is TCBY, a baseball fans shop, a variety of stores, and just down the road is Embassy Suites which has dancing all night.

To show the contrast of Friday's, I picked another restaurant on the River that I am familiar with, Charlie's. Although I have heard people say they liked Charlie's, I myself did not. My friend's and I have been there twice, once for our Junior Prom and another time just for dinner. Both times I went, I came away wondering why I spent my money there. The food was served a la carte; there wasn't a broad selection, it was over priced, the service was slow + unfriendly, the music they played was like that in an aelevator, the atmosphere was "stuffy," and it seemed to be for more of an older and richer crowd. The one positive thing I found to say about Charlie's was that the view of the River was great.

Friday's is a place like no other! It can be a place to go for prom's, on a date, just out with friends, a place to meet people, overall it's just a place to have fun! There is always music playing, football, baseball or basketball on the many televisions, the waitors and waitresses sit down + talk to you, and I personally like the fact that it is a-buzz with loud conversation.

To prove the point that it is a place for many occasions, I have been there with my family for my birthday, on a date, and many times with my friends just for fun. The atmosphere is fun, relaxed, and one that makes you smile. To prove that it is a place for all ages, my parents, siblings, aunts, uncles, and even grandparents love the restaurant. The menu consists of a children's menu, a variety of beverages, and different nationalities of food, and my favorite . . . . a burger for every day of the week!

If anyone ever asks me where the best restaurant in the area is, I will definitely tell them it's Friday's.

To me it is the epitomy of a superb restaurant.

Ode to Friday's!

Arthurs

The windows are aglow and a little steamed up from the lights and people eating inside, the neon sign is flashing the word, "Arthurs," and the green and white striped curtains give the place an "old tavern" look to it. For those who have not figured it out yet, I am describing a restaurant/bar/cafe in Oak Park Square called Arthurs. The "joint" has been passed down from father to son for forty-years.

On the inside, the place is spotless. When you first walk in the partially stained-glass door, to the right of you is an old mahogony bar with a huge mirror hanging behind it, to the left are about thirty-five tables and chairs, and on the entire left wall is what is called "the regulars wall," here there are caricatures of all the customers who have been coming in for over the past forty years. This is one of the most loved things about Arthurs. During the summer there is a patio area available with about fifteen tables and chairs and even a small water fountain.

As my friends and I sat down I was amazed at how friendly everyone was, since this was Oak Park, I expected all of the people to be snobby and full of themselves. The waitors and waitresses were friendly and quick with conversation and to take and serve the orders. It was obvious to tell who the regular's were because the waiters and themselves were joking and carrying on conversation. One of the waitresses, we'll call her Lisa, reminds me of Carla from CHEERS, except Lisa is not as rude. The uniforms for the employees are very casual, a green or white t-shirt with whatever kind of pants they decide to wear.

The menu offers food for everyone, it ranges from a selection of fruits, hamburgers, chicken, seafood, steak, a kids menu, and some choices for those who for some reason or another have to watch what they eat.

While just sitting there enjoying my meal, I could feel he "family" that the employees have among themselves and with their bosses. People joking around like brothers and sisters, talking to each other about how their day was, and they even bring this sense of family into their work and to the customers to make everyone feel welcome and relaxed. On a scale from 1-10, I would have to give ARTHURS a 9:75. The only reason it didn't get a ten is because it takes thiry minutes to get there from my house.

While I was there, I was able to talk to some of the employees and some of the customers and here are some of the things I found out.

Employees (I changed their real names):

How long have you been working here? Joe- for about 5 years I think
. . . Katie- around 5 years . . . Tim- almost 2 years . . . Rachel- only 5
months

Why/what reasons do you like your job? Katie- my boss is great looking (laugh) no seriously, I just love the atmosphere, the people are great
(like a second family) and the pay isn't bad either . . . Tim- I like the fact
that they trust me enough to let me run the kitchen and the bosses listen
to the employees and don't try to use the rank to manipulate us. There
seems to be a "family feeling" between everyone, do you all really get
along that well? Rachel- I've only been here for a little while, but they all
have a way of making you feel comfortable . . . Lynn- the love, honestly, is
so obvious between us that even if one of us quit, we would always be wel-
comed back.. Katie- it definately is real, and I have proof, I live with three
of the people I work with!

Why would you reccommend this job yo anyone who would have
doubts? Lynn- what more could you ask for in a place of employment? I
meet a lot of great people, get paid good money, and it's just fun . . .
Tim- the hours are good, so are the hours and people I work with. Give
me two reasons why you think ARTHURS appeals to people? Joe- what's
not to like? Okay 2 reasons.., the atmosphere is alive and the food is
great . . . Tim- the waiters and waitresses are fun to be around and the
food is the best in Oak Park.

Here are some responses I got from customers: Why do you like coming here? 1- my friends come here all of the time and now I see why they
like it so much, the place just has a great feel about it, it's hip. - I come
here all the tim to talk to Katie and Joe, they are the main reason I come
back, plus the food is pretty good too.

Are you a regular? How many times a week do you come here? - I
come here every single Saturday night to have my beer and just to hang
out - I've been coming here for the last five years, everyone who works
here seems like family . . . I love it! My friends and I usually come here
about twicw a week for dinner, drinks and just to relax after a long day at
work. Do you have any complaints? - yeah, the waitors are too cute and
I'm married, no seriously, how could anyone complain about this place?
- as far as I'm concerned the only day I'll have to complaint is the day
they go out of business, because then I'll have to stay home with my wife.

How would you rate ARTHURS on a scale from 1-10? a 10 no doubt
about it - I give this joint an 11—a big 10

On November 29, I interviewed Walter, one of the owners of Arthurs. As I walked up the ten or twelve steps to his office, the one thing that I remember is how I could still iear all of the commostion and buzz of the restaurant. I reached the sturdy wood door to the office, knocked, and heard deep stern voice telling me to come in. Behind a small desk sat a man in his late thirties or early forties, salt and pepper hair, dark eyes and skin, and a nicely built body. I quickly looked around and saw that there were some photos of his family and one of the entire staff at a picinic last year. There were also trophies and various and awards that Walter and the restaurant has won. As I sat down, we exchanged pleasantries and then I began asking him my questions and here are the replies I got. -How long has Arthurs been in business? The restaurant has been open for around forty years, but I've only been running it for the last ten.

-How personally involved in the restaurant are you? I am very involved, I am here every day except for Tuesday because I need at least one day off. I do share the resposibility with partner Ron and some of the employees have more rank here than others do. For example, Joe, who is my brother-in-law, helps with the hiring of new employees, making the schedule up, and he tells me when things need to be done.

-Where did the name ARTHURS come from? My dad gave it the name, but I think he got it from the top of his head it doesn't symbolize anything.

-What inspired the regulars wall? That was my wife and dad's idea, they said it was a tangible way to let our people know that we do appreciate their loyalty and we do know that they are always there.

-What do you feel keeps the customers coming back? I think the main reason is the treatment they get from the waiters and waitresses. People always tell me how much they love the way they are treated, they say that they feel like part of our ARTHURS family. I personally like our chicken sandwiches aqnd would come back for them.

-The family feeling here is great, how do you think improves business? It improves our business because the people working here truly like their job and cover for each other and that keeps the business running smoothly. I think the attitude the workers have toward each other is brought off on the customers and onto the way they perform their job.

-Why do you feel it is important for the employees to have a say? They aren't just employees, they are like a second family and in a family, if everyone does not get to voice their opinion it won't run as smoothly.

-How do you feel about you wife and brother—in-law working here? It is no different than any other family working together, you seperate business from personal life.

-Do you regret going into this business? Not at all there isn't anything else I would rather be doing.

-How would you rate ARThURS on a scale from 1-10? I would give us an 11...does that sound to crass? No seriously, I would rate us as a 9.5.

-If you could change anything about the restaurant, what would it be? I would like to expand the building but I think it would take away the feeling.

ARTHURS in Oak Park Square is a place that is full of life, energy, and a sense of family. As you can see just by the response of the employees, owner, and some custommers, this is a place people come to timer after time for the food and the atmosphere.

Any preconceived ideas I had were abolished when I walked in the door. The people are not snobs, the prices are reasonable, and you can really feel the sense of family.

From Portfolio 3

A Professional Helper

When Frank Suward says "Baseball is my life" he means it. He also says "I will work as hard as a person can in baseball to succeed". Frank plays extremely above his potential on the ball field. He is also talented when it comes to helping kids off the field. Frank is owner of the newly remolded Western Hills Sports Mall on Thompsion Road. This mall is packed with hundreds of kids, even during the off season. The baseball section at the back of the mall is where Frank works his magic with the youngsters.

"You can not become great at baseball unless you practice every day," Frank said to one of his classes. "The best way to become a ball player is to practice everyday. I have fourteen batting cages open now and you youngsters can use them whenever you want."

When you approach Frank Suwards hitting clinic the sights will amaze even the most sceptic of critics. First of all, it is clean and spacious. Also, the camp is run by professional athletes. The cages form together to make a half circle, with a lobby for tossing and fielding ground balls. The atmosphere is full of childerns desire to win and parents opportunity to brag.

Frank practices everyday with the kids. The first stage of practice is warm ups and stretching by tossing and running. "That is why most athletes do not play high school or college ball, there arms are worn out by not taking the proper percautions before practice." Many people think that his program is excellent because he teaches the players and not some ametuer, "Parents pay good money to have me teach their sons how to play baseball so I will teach the athletes myself".

As practice continues, the youngsters break down into four groups and begin to hit. Frank takes turns watching the future all pro's taking batting practice. He watches a young south pawl in cage three and the machine fires a bullet right past the intimidated boy with an old New York Yankees hat. Frank rushed to the aid of the little boy, they worked together till the problem was solved. While Frank talks with the boy there are various activities boing on. Some hit off a tee, others field grounders, but most of the players just watch Frank with undivided attention and dream about the day that they will be like him.

On the first day of camp a poor family came in to watch practice. "Hello, why aren't you playing?" Frank asked in wounder. When Frank found out the boy could not afford the camp he took money out of his own pocket and paid for it himself. He also bought the boy aquipment so he would feel like he was part of the team. He bought him a Nikoma Kangaroo skinglove and Rawling batting gloves.

"I teach my students everything that I have learned throught the years," Frank Suward said. "At home I think of things to teach the kids. I usually ask other professional how they teach young kids."

Fans watch Frank and his players with enthusiasm, also they wounder how a professional athlete can care so much about kids. One on looker said "Frank Suward plays baseball six months a year and he helps kids out the other six months". He truly lives a baseball life, so when Frank says "Baseball is his life" he definitly means it.

Portfolio 4

Significant Event Essay
June 6, 1991 Graduation

The most significant event in my life was my high school graduation.
Writing this paper helped my accomplish a lot in my writing skills. One
of the most important things writing this paper helped me with was my

*mechanical elements. When writing this essay I followed the out line in
the english book we used in class. When I first did this paper it had a lot
of mechanical elements wrong with it but know I fell that I have
corrected them to the best of my knowledge.*

I awoke on June 6 1991 with a burst of energy. This was the glorious day
that I had waited 12 long years to arrive. During my senior year in high
school, I was filled with anticipation and yet with apprehension. I started
my day by preparing for graduation rehearshal. Sevearal of my good
friends spent the night with me the day before graduation. The morning
was hectic, we were all racing around the house trying to get ready so we
would not be late for rehearsal.

We arrived at E.J. Wallace hall a little after 7:00 A.M.. Once at the hall
we waited along with two-hundred and twelve other anxious students.
Some students came to rehearshal not even knowing if they would graduate. When the principal came with the master list of those who were
graduating, it was a prayer answered from above. Everyone was excited
and happy to know that they had finally arrived at this point in their lives.

We praticed marching into the hail and wafking across the stage. As we
watched others pratice walking across the stage we made jokes and bet on
who would trip going up on stage. All the guys were boasting on how they
were men now and that they would not cry. On the other hand the females
excepted the fact that they might cry as they walked across the stage.

At the end of rehearshal we all said our good-byes because we knew
that after graduation we would be going our seperate ways. After rehearshal we all headed home in order to get ready for graduation.

I started to prepare for the biggest night of my life at 4:30 P.M.. As I
put on my bright red cap and gown, began to feel more like someone
who was about to graduate. Getting dressed was the hardest thing for me
to do because I was thinking about all of the things that could go wrong
such as forgetting my speech and triping when I walked across the stage.

All of the graduating students were out side of E.J. Wallace Hall with
their friends and family at 6:45 P.M. As we waited outside I could see gray
and red gowns and smiling faces everywhere I looked. We laughed,
hugged and took pictures with our loved ones. When the time grew closer
for us to march in, some began to cry, even those that said they would not.

At 7:30 on the evening of June 6, 1991 Dr. D.B. Samuels, my high school
principal, introduced the 1991 East High Senior Class. At that monent I
knew that my life would never be the same. In a span of three hours I
would be leaving one foot in the past and taking one step into the future.

I watched my fellow classmates march into E.J. Wallace Performing Arts Hall, I realized that in less than two minutes I would be taking that final walk to my seat along with my fellow class officers. Dr. Samuels introduced us, to our friends and families who stood and gave us a big welcome. As we proceeded to our seats, my heart was filled wtih joy because I knew that this was going to be one of the best nights of my life.

Once we were all seated, Andrea, our class secretary, gave the invocation. The graduation ceremony moved along like clock work. Sunny, our class president, and Arnold, our vice president, took us on a journey down memory lane. They shared with us all the precious moments; although some were not so precioius. They also shared with the audience the class honors and appreciations. I received several very special awards. One was a plaque which I received a standing ovation and a job well done from everyone.

When Sunny and Arnold were. done giving their speeches it was then time for a presentation by the Board of Education. Our guest speeker was Dr. Winston. Dr. Winston was scheduled to speak for twenty-five long minutes but Dr. Winston decided to give our class a graduation present. His present to us was not to give a speech but to just start handing out the diplomas because he felt we had already waited 12 long years!

As the the first names of the graduating seniors were called I watched as our class begin to take its final walk together. I thought about how some were taking a step towards the future and how some were reflecting on a wasted opportunity during high school. While watching my fellow classmates walk across the stage the hall was filled with joy and happiness. As the list of names grew shorter and the first of the top ten were introduced, I knew that in a matter of minutes I would be receiving my diploma and addressing my fellow class mates for the last time.

Patiently waiting for my name to be called, my school days flew before my eyes. Finally my name was called and I took my final walk as a high school student. I felt like a five-year old learning how to ride a bike for the first time. My belly was filled with butterflies and my legs felt like water under me while my eyes were filled with tears. I slowy reached for my diploma. Once I had my diploma in my hand I said, "THANK YOU GOD".

After all the diplomas were handed out, Mr. Samuels introduced us as the graduating senior class of 1991. It was suddenly my turn to give the final words of wisdom. I slowy walked up to the microphone, which seemed like a mile. I looked out into the many faces looking back at me.

My mouth was dry and my hands started to shake. I just knew that when I opened my mouth no words would come but they did.

"As we come to the conclusion of the graduation ceremony of the East High Senior Class of 1991, I would like to leave you with theses words of wisdom."

> Nothing comes easy
> So don't be deceived
> Hold on to the dreams
> In which you belive

After my speech, I gave permission for the class to stand. I watched my fellow classmates and friends march from their seats. I could feel warm, wet tears rolling down my face as my heart filled with sadness. We had come in as high school seniors and left as newcomers to the real world.

Problem Solution
Room 408

When writing this esay I found it hard for me to write about a problem that I did not truly know about. I decided to writ about a problem I had been having and I know other students here at City University have had. I wrote about the noise in the residence hall. When writing this paper I did not use the writing style in the english book. I felt that it took away what I was trying to write about. As you read my paper you may feel that is a personal experience. I look at it this way something can not be a problem unless you have experienced it or someone else has.

Although I did not follow the books outline I still have a problem that is stated and I also have given some solution that works.

Whith anger, frustration, and curiosity I knocked on the door to room 408. The resident slowly opened her door and said "Hello".

"Hi. I'm Latavia and I live downstairs. I was just womdering if the noise we've been hearing is coming from your room. My roommate arid I have been hearing noise for the past three nights."

"Noise? We have not been making noise. We are just sitting here playing cards and talking." said a girl sitting on the floor with flaming red hair and pop bottle glasses.

"Do you think it might be the girls next door? said the girl who answered the door.

"Who else could it have been? It was not us." said the girl on the floor.

With no answere at the present time I turned and walked back down the hall. I heard a faint whisper in the distance saying, "Oh my god! She can hear us!" Still filled with anger, frustration, and curiosity, I continued to walk back down the steps to my room.

It all began three nights ago. My roommate, Jodi, and I were studing in our room when we heard a strange sound over our heads. At first the noise did not bother us, then the noise grew louder and louder. All of a sudden, the noise died. The room was filled with a quiet humming soud; therefore we continued to study. As the night grew shorter, we prepared for bed. Suddenly, "Grand Central Station" was above our room. "Choo Choo Choo Ching!!" went the noise, over and over again. This time the noise was louder and it began to drive us crazy! Somehow we fell asleep only to encounter the same noise for the next two nights.

Noise, a common dorm life problem, is experienced by almost all residents at one time or another. Either you or someone you know may have at one point, experienced this problem. As a college student, noise can interfere with your ability to study peacefully; it can also cause you to lose sleep as well as interfere with any other activities that require silence. But the question still remains: "What should I do about this problem?"

Upon the third night,. I decided to look into this matter. I was determined to find a solution. I approached the resident who lived next door to me. I knocked and a small voice said, "Come in." I slowly opened the door and went in.

"Hi Stacy! I was just wondering if you have been hearing a strange noise coming above your room."

She replied, "Yah, I sure have been hearing noises. I am trying to study and I connot concentrate with all this racket. I sometimes stand on my bed and bang on the ceiling."

With that response, I further discussed this situation with Jodi. We came up with many solutions, such as banging on the ceiling or turning the radio up. We even thought about running upstairs to their room and knocking on their door and then running away. As much as we wanted to do these action, we decided to try talking to the three young ladies above our room.

The following night we talked to the three girls. they told us that they would try to keep the noise down. They apologized sincerely and we accepted it The anger, frustration and curiosity soon disappeared and every thing turned out fine. Althought my roommate and I were very happy with the out come, we knew that if things did not work out we could have brought this matter into the hands of the Residence Hall Disciplinary System where the referred students have a choice between a Hall Judicial Commission or Administrative hearing. Two other solution that may have worked were talking to our Residence Coordinator or with our Residence Assistant about enforcing quiet hours, courtesy hours and the standard rules of residential community. Which requires its members (students living in the dorms) to behave in a mature and considerate manner.

Profile
What is NSBE

This was one of my best essay I have written this quarter. I liked this type of essay best because I had a subject I could study and I was also could get feed back from different people. I have made no correction or revision to this essay.

What organization here at City University is in pursuit of excellence, dedicated to a better tomorrow, and is helping to develop the techinical and professional skills of its members? I asked my friend Carmen if she knew of any organizations that would fit my description. She told me that NSBE was just the organization I was looking for. She invited me to their next meeting on the following Tuesday. My next question was "What is NSBE?"

Tuesday night I went to the meeting and I found out that NSBE stands for National Society of Black Engineers. Like many other organization here on campus, NSBE holds its meeting like that of a board meeting and stresses higher achievement. For example NSBE is very picky about members being late. Attendance is also very important to them. Although The National Society of Black Engineers meetings are very formal the Executive Board can be more formal.

NSBE was formed 16 years ago here at City University. It is a non-profit organization that is managed by students. Some other general information that Carmen and other members shared was that NSBE was incorpoted in December 1976 in Texas. With over 150 chapters located across the country NSBE operates through a University based structure coordinated through 6 regional zones. City University is in the fourth regional zone.charted The organization is administerd by officers of the National Executive Board with over 5,000 engineering students in accredited degree programs.

The National Society of Black Engineers primary goals are to increase the enrollment of qualified minority students and to reduce their high rate of attrition. Another goal is the promotion, recruitment, retention and successful graduation of blacks in Engineering while trying to stimulate and develop student interest in the various Engineering disciplines. NSBE strives to increase the number of students studying Engineering at the undergraduate and graduate levels. The National Society of Black Engineers also encourages its members to seek advanced degrees in Engineering or related fields, to obtain Professional Engineering Certification, and to promote public awareness of Engineering and opportunities for black and other ethinic minorities.

After getting the information on what NSBE does and what they are about I asked Carmen how the organization goes about accomplishing their goals. Carmen stated in a positive voice that NSBE accomplishes its objectives through the development and implemention of innovation programs conducted at all levels of the organization. Some of the activities that they use to accomplish these objectives are tutorial programs, technical seminars, pre-college programs, and career fairs just to name a few.

After having all my question answered *I* was sold on the fact that The National Society of Black Engineers was indeed the answer to my question. The members of NSBE are truly dedicated to a better tomorrow.

WORKS CITED

NSBE, Organization. Group Interview. 19 Nov. 1991.
Mcann. Carmen. Personal Interview. 21 Nov. 1991.

In class essay
Evaluation: Fix This Mess!

This essay I had a lot of trouble writing. I feel I had a lot of trouble with this because of the limited time we had. In the class room there was a lot of distraction. There was also not enough of time to check the mechanical elements and to make sure all your grammar and other convention were in order.

"FIX THIS MESS!" This is the catchy little phrase that grabed my attention from all the other ads I looked at. I think that the LeKair advertisment is just excellent. It met all the criterias and my standers for an excellent advertisement.

Styling gell and protein conditioning gell that makes your hair manageable and gives it a soft new sophisticated look New LeKair styling gel,

the hair care product of the future. This is the message I got when looking at the advertisment for LeKair styling gell and protein conditioning.
This is the type of message I was looking for it is catchy, applies to the
LeKair product, it is also concise and complette. Another little phrases
that grabed my attention was "LeKair Styling Gell and Protein
Conditioning Gel Do Wonders For Your Hair!" This again is also concise
and complete and to the point. It tells you what the product is and what
it is used for and also what it can do for you.

The color in this advertisement is just great and it works well with the
picture and the image it is giveing. The contrast between the two
wemen's hair is just wonderfull. I think that the coloration between the
two tells every thing there is to know about what LeKair can do. The texture of the hair is also very improtant. It makes you wonder what LeKair
can do for your hair. The look on the women in yellow face also moti-
vates the reader to try LeKair Another reason why I think that it is a
great picture is because if you ever ran across someone who's hair
looked better than yours you would mostly pat your hair and say to yourself "Wow my hair looks bad compared to her's"

The eye of appeal of this advertisement is also wonderful. I like the
way they have set up the four different kinds of conditioner and styling
gel's at the bottom of the ad. This lets the reader know what kind of con-
tainer the product comes in. Even the coloring of the containers are
eye-catching.

Alround this advertisement is just great and it met all my criteria.
This ad was very colorfull concise and complete. It was also colorfull
and eye-catching.

Appendix C
TABULATION OF VOTES ON SAMPLE TEXTS

Mid-Term Norming Session Votes (Pass/Fail)

	Pops (P/F)	Anguish (P/F)	Belle (P/F)	Gramma Sally (P/F)
Team A	15/2	0/17	17/0	6/11
Team B-1	3/2	0/5	5/0	3/2
Team B-2	7/0	0/7	7/0	4/2
Team C	20/2	4/18	22/0	11/11
Vote Totals	45/6	4/47	51/0	24/26
Percentages (rounded)	88/12	8/92	100/0	48/52

End-Term Norming Session Votes (Pass/Fail)

	Portfolio 1 (P/F)	Portfolio 2 (P/F)	Portfolio 3 (P/F)	Portfolio 4 (P/F)
Team A	13/0	10/3	0/13	1/12
Team B-1	6/0	3/3	2/4	0/6
Team B-2	7/0	4/3	0/7	0/7
Team C	21/0	16/5	4/17	0/21
Vote Totals	47/0	33/14	6/41	1/46
Percentages (rounded)	100/0	70/30	13/87	2/98

Appendix D
SAMPLE INTERVIEW QUESTIONS

1. As you look back on last quarter's Portfolio Program, what stands out in your mind?

2. If your experiences in the Portfolio Program changed your way of thinking about or handling things, describe how.

3. If norming and trio discussions affected your teaching, whether inside or outside of class, describe how.

4. Approximately what percentage of the time did you give your students the grades agreed upon for them by your trio?

5. [follow up on any key terms that arise, asking for clarification: *Reliability, Validity, Negotiation, Objectivity, Autonomy, Community, Fairness,* etc.]

6. As you look back on norming and trio sessions, are there any moments that stand out for you? Describe them. What was going on? What was your role? How successfully do you feel the people involved handled the situation?

7. As you reflect on norming and trio sessions, do you recall moments in which you changed your mind about something: an evaluation, a criterion, a standard, etc.? Describe the process of changing your mind.

8. Did you try to change others' minds? What about? How did you do that? How successful do you think you were? How do you know?

9. [Ask about specific moments of evident conflict and/or transformation that I observed in norming and/or trio sessions. Allow interviewee to look at relevant passages in the transcripts.]

10. f you could change anything about the way the program was run—or the way it will be run next time—what would you change? What would you do differently?

Appendix E
KEY TO TRANSCRIPT CITATIONS

The table below shows the full and abbreviated names of the transcripts from which I drew excerpts in my data analysis and in composing this book. These abbreviations appear after each excerpt, followed by the transcript line number at which that quotation began. Though readers do not have access to my transcripts, I thought it might be helpful to them to be able to gauge at what relative point in various conversations particular quotations occurred.

Note that in citing transcripts as sources for quotations, I use the following conventions for abbreviation:

- First I name the group or individual who was recorded: "C 6" refers to trio C-6; "A" refers to team A. Recordings of individual interviews are identified by interviewees' pseudonyms ("Sandra," for instance).
- Next I show at what point in the sequence of events the recording was made. "Mid" refers to midterm, when individual essays were discussed; "Port" refers to the end of the term, when sample texts were portfolios. If I conducted more than one interview with an individual, a number indicates which interview is being cited. (I interviewed participants from one to three times each, depending on their availability.)
- Then I indicate which type of event was recorded. "Norm" refers to a norming session; "Trio" indicates a trio session.

Transcript Name	Abbreviation for Citations
Norming	
Team A midterm norming	A Mid Norm
Team A portfolio norming	A Port Norm
Team C midterm norming	C Mid Norm
Team C portfolio norming	C Port Norm

Trios

Trio A-1 midterm meeting	A-1 Mid Trio
Trio A-1 portfolio meeting	A-1 Port Trio
Trio C-6 midterm meeting	C-6 Mid Trio
Trio C-6 portfolio meeting	C-6 Port Trio

Administrators' Pre-Portfolio (End-Term) Norming Meeting	Admin Pre-Port Norm

Interviews

Emily Interview 1	Emily 1
Emily Interview 2	Emily 2
Emily Interview 3	Emily 3
Kevin Interview 1	Kevin 1
Kevin Interview 2	Kevin 2
Kevin Interview 3	Kevin 3
Laura Interview	Laura
Martin Interview 1	Martin 1
Martin Interview 2	Martin 2
Rhonda Interview	Rhonda
Sandra Interview	Sandra
Ted Interview 1	Ted 1
Ted Interview 2	Ted 2
Terri Interview 1	Terri 1
Terri Interview 2	Terri 2
Terri Interview 3	Terri 3
Veronica Interview 1	Veronica 1
Veronica Interview 2	Veronica 2

REFERENCES

Agar, Michael H. 1980. *The Professional Stranger.* New York: Academic Press.
———. 1986. *Speaking of Ethnography.* Beverly Hills, Calif.: Sage.
Allen, Michael S. 1995. Valuing Differences: Portnet's First Year. *Assessing Writing* 2 (1): 67–89.
Axelrod, Rise B., and Charles Cooper. 1991. *The St. Martin's Guide to Writing.* Short 3d ed. New York: St. Martin's.
Barritt, Loren, Patricia L. Stock, and Francelia Clark. 1986. Researching Practice: Evaluating Assessment Essays. *College Composition and Communication* 38:315–27.
Baxter Magolda, Marcia B. 2001. *Making Their Own Way: Narratives for Transforming Higher Education to Promote Self-Development.* Sterling, VA: Stylus.
Belanoff, Pat, and Peter Elbow. 1991. Using Portfolios to Increase Collaboration and Community in a Writing Program. In *Portfolios: Process and Product,* edited by P. Belanoff and M. Dickson. Portsmouth, N.H.: Boynton/Cook (Heinemann).
Berlin, James A. 1996. *Rhetorics, Poetics, and Cultures.* Urbana, Ill.: National Council of Teachers of English.
Broad, Bob 1997. Reciprocal Authorities in Communal Writing Assessment: Constructing Textual Value within a "New Politics of Inquiry". *Assessing Writing* 4 (2): 133–67.
———. 2000. Pulling Your Hair Out: Crises of Standardization in Communal Writing Assessment. *Research in the Teaching of English* 35 (2): 213–60.
Broad, Robert L. 1994a. "Portfolio Scoring": A Contradiction in Terms. In *New Directions in Portfolio Assessment,* edited by L. Black, Donald A. Daiker, Jeffrey Sommers, and Gail Stygall. Portsmouth, N.H.: Boynton/Cook (Heinemann).
———. 1994b. Working in the City: Building Community and Negotiating Difference in a Portfolio Assessment Program. Ph.D. diss., Miami University (Ohio).
Carter, James R. 1999. *The Individual Map User.* Website. http://lilt.ilstu.edu/jrcarter/icamuc/individuals.html.
Charmaz, Kathy. 2000. Grounded Theory: Objectivist and Constructivist Methods. In *Handbook of Qualitative Research,* edited by N. K. Denzin and Y. S. Lincoln. Thousand Oaks, Calif.: Sage.
Charney, Davida. 1984. The Validity of Using Holistic Scoring to Evaluate Writing: A Critical Overview. *Research in the Teaching of English* 18:65–81.
Cronbach, Lee J. 1990. *Essentials of Psychological Testing.* 5th ed. New York: Harper.

Delandshere, Ginette, and Anthony R. Petrosky. 1998. Assessment of Complex Performances: Limitations of Key Measurement Assumptions. *Educational Researcher* 27 (2): 14–24.

Diederich, Paul B., John W. French, and Sydell T. Carlton. 1961. *Factors in Judgments of Writing Ability* (ETS Research Bulletin 61-15). Princeton: Educational Testing Service.

Elbow, Peter. 2001. Conversation with author, Oxford, Ohio, 5 October.

Elbow, Peter, and Pat Belanoff. 1991. State University of New York at Stony Brook Portfolio-based Evaluation Program. In *Portfolios: Process and Product,* edited by P. Belanoff and M. Dickson. Portsmouth, N.H.: Boynton/Cook (Heinemann).

Faigley, Lester. 1989. Judging Writing, Judging Selves. *College Composition and Communication* 40 (8): 395–412.

———. 1992. *Fragments of Rationality: Postmodernity and the Subject of Composition.* Pittsburgh: University of Pittsburgh Press.

Fife, Jane Mathison, and Peggy O'Neill. 2001. Moving Beyond the Written Comment: Narrowing the Gap Between Response Practice and Research. *College Composition and Communication* 53 (2): 300–21.

Flower, Linda. 1989. Cognition, Context, and Theory Building. *College Composition and Communication* 40 (3): 282–311.

Glaser, Barney G., and Anselm L. Strauss. 1967. *The Discovery of Grounded Theory: Strategies for Qualitative Research.* Chicago: Aldine.

Guba, Egon. 1978. *Toward a Methodology of Naturalistic Inquiry in Educational Evaluation.* Los Angeles: University of California Graduate School of Education.

Guba, Egon G., and Yvonna S. Lincoln. 1989. *Fourth Generation Evaluation.* Newbury Park, Calif.: Sage.

Gubrium, Jaber F., and James A. Holstein. 2000. Analyzing Interpretive Practice. In *Handbook of Qualitative Research,* edited by N. K. Denzin and Y. S. Lincoln. Thousand Oaks, Calif.: Sage.

Hacker, Diana. 1992. *A Writer's Reference.* 2d ed. New York: St. Martin's.

Huot, Brian A. 1993. The Influence of Holistic Scoring Procedures on Reading and Rating Student Essays. In *Validating Holistic Scoring for Writing Assessment: Theoretical and Empirical Foundations,* edited by M. M. Williamson and B. A. Huot. Cresskill, N.J.: Hampton.

———. 1996. Toward a New Theory of Writing Assessment. *College Composition and Communication* 47 (4): 549–66.

———. 2002 *(Re)Articulating Writing Assessment for Teaching and Learning.* Logan: Utah State University Press.

Illinois Standard Achievement Test of Writing. 2002. Website. http://www.isbe.net/assessment/writeperfdef.html.

Kushner, Tony. 1996. *Angels in America: A Gay Fantasia on National Themes (Part Two: Perestroika, Revised Version).* New York: Theatre Communications Group.

Messick, Samuel. 1989. Validity. In *Educational Measurement,* edited by R. L. Linn. Washington, D.C.: National Council on Measurement in Education.

Miles, Matthew B., and A. M. Huberman. 1984. *Qualitative Data Analysis: A Sourcebook of New Methods.* Beverly Hills, Calif.: Sage.

Moss, Pamela A. 1992. Shifting Conceptions of Validity in Educational Measurement: Implications for Performance Assessment. *Review of Educational Research* 62 (3): 229–258.

———. 1994. Can There Be Validity Without Reliability? *Educational Researcher* 23 (2): 5–12.

———. 1996. Enlarging the Dialogue in Educational Measurement: Voices from Interpretive Research Traditions. *Educational Researcher* 25 (1): 20–28, 43.

Neal, Michael. 2002. What Validity Is and Is Not and Why That's Important. Paper read at Conference on College Composition and Communication, Chicago, Illinois.

North, Stephen. 1987. *The Making of Knowledge in Composition: Portrait of an Emerging Field.* Upper Montclair, N.J.: Boynton/Cook.

Patton, Michael Quinn. 1990. *Qualitative Evaluation and Research Methods.* 2d ed. Newbury Park, Calif.: Sage.

Pula, Judith J., and Brian A. Huot. 1993. A Model of Background Influences on Holistic Raters. In *Validating Holistic Scoring for Writing Assessment: Theoretical and Empirical Foundations,* edited by M. M. Williamson and B. A. Huot. Cresskill, N.J.: Hampton.

Reynolds, Nedra. 1990. Issues of Consensus, Authority, and Resistance: A Study/Story of a Rater-Training Session. Paper read at University of New Hampshire Conference on the Writing Process, October 5–7, Durham, New Hampshire.

Sosnoski, James J. "The Psycho-Politics of Error." Pre-Text 10.1-2 (1989): 33–52.

Strauss, Anselm L. 1987. *Qualitative Analysis for Social Scientists.* New York: Cambridge University Press.

Strauss, Anselm, and Juliet Corbin. 1994. Grounded Theory Methodology: An Overview. In *Handbook of Qualitative Research,* edited by N. K. Denzin and Y. S. Lincoln. Thousand Oaks, Calif.: Sage.

——— . 1998. *Basics of Qualitative Research.* Thousand Oaks, Calif.: Sage.

Walvoord, Barbara E., and Virginia Johnson Anderson. 1998. *Effective Grading: A Tool for Learning and Assessment.* San Francisco: Jossey-Bass.

White, Edward M. 1994. *Teaching and Assessing Writing.* 2d ed. San Francisco: Jossey-Bass.

Wiggins, Grant. 1994. The Constant Danger of Sacrificing Validity to Reliability: Making Writing Assessment Serve Writers. *Assessing Writing* 1 (1): 129–39.

Williams, Joseph M. 1981. The Phenomenology of Error. *College Composition and Communication* 32 (May): 152–68.

Williamson, Michael M. 1993. An Introduction to Holistic Scoring: The Social, Historical, and Theoretical Context for Writing Assessment. In *Validating*

Holistic Scoring for Writing Assessment: Theoretical and Empirical Foundations, edited by M. M. Williamson and B. A. Huot. Cresskill, N.J.: Hampton.

Yancey, Kathleen Blake. 1999. Looking Back as We Look Forward: Historicizing Writing Assessment. *College Composition and Communication* 50 (3): 483–503.

INDEX

BOB BROAD is associate professor of English at Illinois State University, where he teaches graduate and undergraduate courses in writing assessment, research methods, pedagogics of literature and composition, and other aspects of English Studies. His research has appeared in the journals *Research in the Teaching of English, Assessing Writing, Works and Days,* and *African American Review* and in the collections *New Directions in Portfolio Assessment* (Boynton/Cook 1994) and *Preparing a Nation's Teachers: Model Programs for English and Foreign Languages* (MLA 1999). Bob also runs Just Words Consulting Group, which provides clients with guidance on authentic writing assessment, technology and (teaching) writing, and other aspects of literacy education. In his own Justoons Recording Studios, Bob recently recorded a CD of songs he wrote over the last twenty years; if you ask nicely, he'll probably give you a copy of your very own.